Jurisdiction

This book takes its cue from the observation that jurisdiction – as the speech of law – articulates or proclaims law. Without jurisdiction the law would be speechless, without authority and authorisation. So too would be critics who approach the law or want to live lawfully. As a field of legal knowledge and legal practice, jurisdiction is concerned with the modes of authority and the manner of the authorisation of law. It encompasses the broadest questions of the authority and the founding of legal order as well as the minutest detail of the ordering of the business of the administration and adjudication of justice. It gives us both the point of articulation of law and the technological means of the expression of law. It gives us, too, the understanding of the limits of the authority of law, as well as the resources for engaging with the plurality of laws, and the means of engaging in lawful behaviour. A critical approach to law through the forms of authority and action in law provides a means of engaging with the quality of relations created and maintained through law and a means of taking responsibility for the practices of jurisdiction (and what is done in the name of the law).

Jurisdiction provides a critical, and historically grounded, elaboration of the key themes of jurisdiction. It does so by offering students and scholars of law a form of critical engagement with the technologies, devices and forms of jurisdictional ordering. It shows how the common law has authorised legal relations and bound persons, places, and events to the body of law. It offers a number of resources and engagements of jurisdiction on the basis that a jurisprudence of jurisdiction, if it is anything, engages forms of human relation.

Shaunnagh Dorsett is Associate Professor at the Faculty of Law, University of Technology, Sydney. She writes at the intersections of legal history, native title and jurisprudence.

Shaun McVeigh is Associate Professor at the Melbourne Law School, University of Melbourne. He has research interests in the fields of jurisprudence, legal ethics and health care.

Critical Approaches to Law

The Critical Approaches to Law series aims to secure a place for critical, interdisciplinary, and/or theoretical work on the law curriculum. Each book provides a critical approach to a particular legal topic: whether this is an issue or theme within law or legal study, a disciplinary or sub-disciplinary area, a specific legal institution, a significant text, case or piece of legislation, an event, a person, or a specific approach to, or tradition of, law. The series encourages critical thought in and about law through a range of clear and accessible texts that are suitable for higher level undergraduates and postgraduates, as well as academic and practising lawyers who are seeking critical work in their area.

Other books in this series:

Property
Meanings, Histories, Theories
Margaret Davies

Regulation of the Voluntary Sector
Freedom and Security in an Era of Uncertainty
Mark Sidel

Forthcoming titles in this series:

Capital Punishment and Political Sovereignty
Adam Thurshwell

International Development
Sundhya Pahuja, Jennifer Beard and Ruth Buchanan

Jurisdiction

Shaunnagh Dorsett
and Shaun McVeigh

Routledge
Taylor & Francis Group
a GlassHouse Book

First published 2012
by Routledge
2 Park Square, Milton Park, Abingdon, Oxon OX14 4RN

Simultaneously published in the USA and Canada
by Routledge
711 Third Avenue, New York, NY 10017

A GlassHouse book

Routledge is an imprint of the Taylor & Francis Group, an informa business

© 2012 Shaunnagh Dorsett and Shaun McVeigh

The right of Shaunnagh Dorsett and Shaun McVeigh to be
identified as authors of this work has been asserted by them in
accordance with sections 77 and 78 of the Copyright, Designs and
Patents Act 1988.

British Library Cataloguing in Publication Data
A catalogue record for this book is available from the British Library

Library of Congress Cataloging in Publication Data
Dorsett, Shaunnagh.
    Jurisdiction / Shaunnagh Dorsett and Shaun McVeigh.
        p. cm.
    Includes bibliographical references and index.
    1. Jurisdiction. I. McVeigh, Shaun. II. Title.
    K2226.D67 2012
    347'.012—dc23   2011051205

ISBN: 978–0–415–47163–3 (hbk)
IBSN: 978–0–415–47165–7 (pbk)
ISBN: 978–0–203–11543–5 (ebk)

Typeset in Times New Roman
by Keystroke, Station Road, Codsall, Wolverhampton

MIX
Paper from
responsible sources
FSC
www.fsc.org   FSC® C004839

Printed and bound in Great Britain by
TJ International Ltd, Padstow, Cornwall

Contents

Acknowledgements

Over the years of writing about jurisdiction we have incurred many debts to colleagues and friends. In particular, we would like to thank Olivia Barr, Christine Black, Peter Goodrich, Ian Hunter, Bill MacNeil, Jeffrey Minson, Anne Orford, Sundhya Pahuja and Peter Rush, for the conversations, the critique, the feedback and the support. Many other colleagues, too numerous to mention, have helped so much. We are sure you know who you are. Shaunnagh Dorsett benefited in particular from the Melbourne Law School International Visiting Scholar program in 2009. At Routledge, we would like to thank Colin Perrin for allowing us to write and finish with jurisdiction, and Melanie Fortmann-Brown for the encouragement to actually finish.

On a personal note, we would especially like to thank Livingstone McVeigh-Go, George Lafferty and Ann Genovese. Livingstone, in particular, has grown up with jurisdiction and has done so with such grace.

Chapter 1

Introduction

We will have lived in a world of jurisdiction. We are brought into life and set in motion according to the authority of law, our conduct is shaped according to civil order, and our conscience created and turned to political faith in law and community. Jurisdictional thinking, so to speak, gives legal form to life and life to law. In the world of St Augustine, it gives us the structure of our existence. In the idioms of European traditions of law we cannot move but for the work of jurisdiction. Our deaths, too, will be marked by questions of jurisdiction and care of law (or its lack).

Consider some forms that a jurisdiction might take. The Popes of the medieval Catholic Church exercised a jurisdiction over the whole world – its peoples and lands. The authority of the Pope and the Holy Roman Emperor was expressed in terms of a universal jurisdiction. In part, this was a matter of divine authority and in part a matter of *imperium* and *dominion* – of rule (power) and property. By the Papal Bull *Romanus Pontifex*, 8 January 1455 (Davenport 1917: 23–24), Alexander VI granted the Monarch and heirs of Castile and Leon (now modern Spain) the exclusive right to acquire territory, to trade in, or even to approach the lands lying west of the meridian situated 100 leagues west of any of the Azores or Cape Verde Islands, limited only by existing claims from Christian princes. In this way the world, and the yet to be discovered New World, was divided and contested (Tuck 1979). Or, consider too the jurisdictional re-arrangement of the relation between the English crown and the Roman Church. In 1533 the Act of Appeals 24 Hen VIII, c 12 effectively secured the split between the Church of Rome and the Church of England. It declared in the preamble that England was an empire and forbade all appeals to the Pope in Rome on religious or other matters, making the king the final authority in all such matters in England, Wales and all other English possessions. The following year, the Supremacy Act 26 Hen VIII c 1 confirmed that Henry had always been the head of the

Church of England. The removal of the jurisdiction of the Church of Rome marked one of the decisive formations of English sovereignty. Consider too the work of the courts of the common law. In *Le Case de Tanistry* (1608) Davis 28 it was determined that the *Brehon* law (the Irish common law as understood by the English) had been abolished by the introduction of the English common law, and that henceforth relations of kinship and to land were displaced by English law. This was a moment of jurisdictional force that marked and continued to mark the colonial inheritance of law (Dorsett 2002). Consider also *Prohibition del Roy* 12 Co Rep 63, 65; 77 ER 1342, in which Coke asserted the power of the judges to decide legal disputes before and over that of the king. James I claimed he could also could resolve legal disputes because 'the law is founded on reason, and that he and the others had reason as well as judges'. Coke replied that 'true it was that God had endowed his Majesty with excellent science, and great endowments of nature; but his Majesty was not learned in the laws of the realm of England, and causes . . . are not to be decided by natural reason but by the artificial reason of the law, which law is an act which requires long study and experience' (12 Co Rep 63, 65; 77 ER 1342, 1343; Cover 1993: 183). This assertion of common law jurisdiction is treated in modern law as one of the bases for the separation of powers.

Consider the jurisdiction of the student scholar at the University of Bologna. In 1153, the Holy Roman Emperor Frederick Barbarossa granted privileges and jurisdictions to teachers at Bologna by the imperial decree *Authentica Habita*. It allowed for each student scholar to recognise the jurisdiction of his professor in all matters affecting him; to claim imperial protection to travel to study; and a right not to be punished for the non-payment of the debts of other students. Students could choose between the jurisdiction of their teachers or of their bishops. This decree is today treated as the foundation document of the University of Bologna, and is often thought of as a statement of academic freedom and the foundation of legal study as a matter of conscience. The grant was also an act of imperial authority made in recognition that the jurists of Bologna had delivered legal opinions in favour of the emperor against local laws (Douzinas 2007: vi–viii; Barr 2010).

Many modern jurisdictional forms inherit, repeat and develop older expressions of law and legal relations. Consider the emergence of the doctrine of the responsibility to protect in international law (Orford 2011). If the primary reason for the state is to protect its population, the doctrine of responsibility to protect allows that if a state fails in this duty then the international community should take up the responsibility. It marks out a distinct jurisdictional authority for executive action within the United Nations. Anne Orford has pointed to the way in which the jurisdictional arrangements imagined by the responsibility to protect doctrine are similar to those of the medieval Holy Roman Empire. States have responsibility for populations within a named territory, the United Nations has responsibility and jurisdiction over the international community as a whole (Orford 2011: 27) Consider too the exercise of jurisdiction of courts in the international domain. Take the decision by the government of Israel in the matter of the seizure and trial of the German Adolf Eichmann to take up a jurisdiction, to take responsibility and exercise authority, in the matter of 'crimes against humanity'. The issue became one of whether the state of Israel could take jurisdiction. The trial was for acts committed outside the bounds of the state, against a person who was not an Israeli citizen, by a person who acted in the course of duty on behalf of a foreign country, and for acts committed before Israel existed (*Government of Israel v Adolph Eichmann* 36 IRL 5, [8], Dist Court Jerusalem, affd 36 ILR 277, reprinted in (1962) 56 *Am J Int'l L* 805). The court asserted the power or right to punish because 'the crimes . . . afflicted the whole of mankind and shocked the conscience of nations [and] are grave offences against the law of nations itself. . . . The authority and jurisdiction to try crimes under international law are *universal*' (at [12]). We return to the Eichmann trial in Chapter 7.

Consider too the meeting of laws and the impoverished jurisdictional forms of the acknowledgement of indigenous laws by former 'settler colonies' such as Australia, Canada, New Zealand, South Africa and the United States. Australia's legal judgments and laws have given effect to forms of 'native title' that recognise indigenous laws within the legal ordering of the state. They did so reprising the jurisdictional questions in the *Case of Tanistry* (*Mabo v State of Queensland (No 2)* (1992) 175 CLR 1; Dorsett 2002), a matter we return to in Chapter 6.

Here is another formulation of jurisdiction from the work of Seamus Heaney. In his essay 'Feeling into Words', Heaney writes of the ways in which he found his 'voice' as a poet (Heaney 2002). In a number of formulations to which we will return, Heaney points to the way in which in technique 'entails the watermarking of your essential patterns of perception, voice and thought into the touch and texture of your lines; it is that whole creative effort of the mind's and body's resources to bring the meaning of experience within the jurisdiction of form' (Heaney 2002: 47). It is with the jurisdiction of form as much as forms of jurisdiction that we make our critical approach to law.

Perhaps, however, this is not entirely the correct way or place to start. Jurisdiction might be viewed as the most technical and prosaic ordering of legal authority. Jurisdictional knowledge is, in a sense, the practical knowledge of how to do things with law. Its formulations are part of the technique and craft of legal ordering and the art of creating legal relations. Its everyday concerns are concerns that have been around for centuries. They turn on matters of granting authority to act, establishing courts and tribunals, issuing summons to attend court, filing documents for hearings and exchanging arguments about the proper time and place to hear a case. A jurisdiction might delimit the scope of authority, determine the technical means of its representation or adjudicate on the proper form of lawful relations. It could also set in motion disputes about how to regulate the internet, how to manage personal and family relations in places governed by many rival claims to authority; and so on. In this orientation, jurisdiction takes on importance in daily life. It tells us how to do things with and against law. It also opens a domain of thought, or a jurisprudence, concerned with how to live with law and how to create and engage lawful relations.

A starting point for our thinking about jurisdiction comes from Peter Rush, who writes that jurisdiction 'refers us first and foremost to the power and authority to speak in the name of the law and only subsequently to the fact that law is stated – and stated to be someone or something' (Rush 1997: 150). Similarly, Coke (one of the few common law jurists to try to define jurisdiction) stated that 'jurisdiction is the authority to decide or give judgment among parties concerning actions to be taken over people and property . . . Jurisdiction is the power to give judgment on a public matter, and is instituted by necessity' (Coke 1644: Preface B and *Case of Marshalsea* 10 Co Rep 69). From this, and from the word 'jurisdiction' itself, we can take two things. First, jurisdiction connotes authority. Second, it is an act of speaking – of declaring the law. Jurisdiction is derived from the Latin *ius dicere* – literally to speak the law. Thus, jurisdiction is the practice of pronouncing the law. It declares the existence of law and the authority to speak in the name of the law. Coke himself excerpted this quote from the medieval jurist Azo. However, when he did so, Coke left out a few words at the end: 'and of establishing equity'. This is interesting because it reminds us that there are rival forms of authority and rival positions, as well as the contested nature of thinking with conscience (Goodrich 2008).[1]

Jurisdiction is, however, more than simply pronouncing existing law. In some formulations jurisdiction inaugurates law itself. Thus, to exercise jurisdiction is to bring law into existence, although as we shall see it does so in a certain way and by certain means. We can, therefore, consider jurisdiction as the first question of law, because it asks whether law exists at all, and thus determines what can properly be considered law. It gives us a way of authorising law – of saying that something is lawful or belongs to law – only subsequently is it declared what that law is. While this is a start, however, there is much more that needs to be said. Jurisdiction engages law in a variety of ways. Perhaps most importantly, it both gives us the form and shape of law and the idiom of law.

Jurisdictional thought and practice provides the visible (and occasionally invisible) forms that law takes. Today the most obvious form of legal ordering is that of the sovereign territorial state. We are perhaps used to sovereignty as a political idea – it is the source of power and authority – but we pay much less attention to the material legal forms of sovereign, state and territory. We have become used to the representation of the authority of the sovereign, and of law, as abstract and virtual. In Western idioms, law is often viewed as a matter of right represented as rule or principle. In early modern times, authority was often represented in a material way. An obvious example is that of the king who in fact represented authority both through his actual person and through his institutional/legal form (Kantorowicz 1957: 336–342). We still do this in modern times, we just do not treat material representations as having legal significance. One example might be the flag or the map, both of which materially represent the nation and hence the authority of the nation state. We leave invisible the legal form. One of the observations developed in this book is that the abstractness and immateriality of law is greatly exaggerated. It is important to take disputes over the material form of law seriously.

Jurisdictional thinking gives us a distinct way of representing authority because it gives us the voice or idiom of law. This is the 'diction' part of the term 'jurisdiction'. When we think about an idiom we are thinking about the language and style of talking about law. Talk of jurisdiction does not simply describe law from the outside – it gives us the ways and means of talking about and practicing law. We might think of the practice of law as the craft of law. While we discuss this in more detail in Chapter 4, for present purposes the terms 'practice' and 'craft' simply indicate that jurisdiction is not just a descriptive concept – that jurisdiction, through institutions, actively works to produce something. So, as practices, the idioms of jurisdiction concern the means of creating and ordering law. For example, they provide the practical organisation of the business of the courts and the management of the scope or extent of authority to judge. The practical organisation of the courts can be thought of as part of the technological or procedural ordering of law. Without such modes of thinking about law there would be no way of engaging with law as a practical activity with purpose. However, while jurisdictional thinking is never less than practical it is also and always something more. It is not just about which court to go to start a legal action, it is also about what is to count as a legal action and how a legal action can be characterized as belonging to law. Our modern understanding of jurisdiction tends to the technical. If you look at the textbooks of law, the law relating to jurisdiction appears in two ways. It appears first as a matter of the administration of justice and the ordering of courts, and second as a concern of conflict, of conflict of laws and conflicts of jurisdiction. Both ways assume the existence of law (as all law texts do in some way) and that the only question to be asked is which court administers that law or which law or court prevails in a conflict? In this book we have slowed down this way of thinking in order to get a surer sense of what is at issue in matters of jurisdiction. Jurisdiction is the first question of law and the first point of engagement for a critical approach to law.

As the first question jurisdiction asks is whether law exists at all, the question of which law follows on. So one form of critical engagement with law does not begin with the question of 'What is law?' or even 'What is justice?', it begins with the practical questions of: 'Under which law?', 'Who will decide?' and 'Who will interpret?'. Only then can we move to questions of 'How do we live with law?' and 'How do we live justly with law?'. Considered as questions of jurisdiction these questions become ones of lawfulness – of what it means to belong to, and to live with, law. Lawfulness, then, is a material practice, concerned with how we inhabit the world. In this book, the critical response to law we develop responds to these questions in terms of conduct. If jurisdictional thinking teaches us anything about contemporary forms and idioms of law, it is that the critical engagement of law takes place not just at the level of ideas or practice, but also at the level of conduct. Our motto then for this book might be that there is no talk of law without speech – and there is no consideration of lawful speech without form.

Chapter by chapter

Chapter 2 considers how we engage with law through jurisdiction. In jurisdiction might be found questions of the inauguration of law – its value and validity – and its articulation. So key questions might be 'Who speaks and who listens? and 'How are representation of the orders of law engendered through jurisdiction?'. This chapter sets out a number of key ideas about jurisdiction. It looks at jurisdiction both as a practice of law and as a distinct form of critical engagement with law.

Chapter 3 asks how we can understand jurisdiction as a form of authority. This chapter engages with relations between sovereignty, territory and jurisdiction. It emphasises the importance of the twin inheritance of the medieval forms of spiritual and temporal jurisdictions. We also consider the plurality of jurisdictional forms. In doing this, we examine some of the resources of a jurisprudence capable of living with and re-ordering forms of common law authority.

Chapter 4 looks at how we tie the institutional practices of law to the conduct of lawful relations. This chapter is concerned with how the technologies of jurisdiction are engaged in the creation and arrangement of legal relations, and with how the technologies of jurisdiction give us the form of law and engage with the representation of law. Here we draw out the ways in which the technologies of jurisdiction represent the body of law and engage lawful relations. We suggest that without an account of the technologies of jurisdiction there is no way of tying the institutional practices of law to the conduct of lawful relations – whether critical or doctrinal.

Chapters 5, 6 and 7 put into practice some of the ideas of jurisdiction considered in the previous four chapters. Each chapter does this through a short series of studies which take up aspects of authority, authorisation and the technologies of jurisdiction. Each chapter is organised around a key mode of jurisdiction: persons, places and events. Each fundamentally asks the same question: 'How do we create and maintain lawful relations?'. So Chapter 5 asks how we make a legal person. This is investigated through the example of assisted suicide, and shows how even subjects as embedded in ethical dispute as the right to life (or to die), such as assisted suicide and euthanasia, are shaped through rival understandings of jurisdiction. We provide a particular example of a way of articulating (expressing) and conducting lawful relations jurisdictionally. In so doing, this chapter is particularly concerned with forms of personal jurisdiction and the law of persons.

Chapter 6 continues by asking how relations of place are articulated and expressed with law. What happens when sovereignty is the only language of authority and territorial sovereignty is the dominant mode of jurisdiction? Here we look at specific practices and the ways of understanding the meeting of laws as a jurisdictional concern. We concentrate here on the meeting of indigenous and non-indigenous jurisdictions in Australia. We do so in order to draw out the sense of the meeting of jurisdictions as both a matter of technical ordering and of the conduct of lawful relations.

Chapter 7 moves from persons and places to events. We consider how events or activities become engaged in law. This chapter examines the forms of community and address of the jurisdictions that make up the international domain. We consider the mode and manner in which the contemporary jurisdictions of the international jurisdictions have created new political, legal and ethical forms of international life. We look to the quality of the international as a meeting place of law – a meeting place among or between nations. The meeting point provides a point of order from which to examine the way events cohere in law.

In the final chapter, we bring the jurisprudence of jurisdiction into relation with critical accounts of jurisdiction. By way of conclusion, we offer an account of the repertories of jurisdiction as a practice of responsibility for the forms of law. In order to do so, we return to the offices of jurist, jurisprudent and critic. The critical approach to law presented here is shaped around the ways in which it is possible to take responsibility for law through attending to the practices of jurisdiction.

Notes

1   Equity here refers of course not to Chancery, but to civil law – in other words for Coke equity refers to the rival authority of Rome.

References

Barr, O. (2010) 'A Moving Theory: Remembering the Office of Scholar', *Law Text Culture* 14: 40–56.

Coke, E. (1644) *The Fourth Part of the Institutes of the Laws of England: Concerning the Jurisdiction of Courts*, London: W. Lee and D. Parkman.

Cover, R. (1993) 'The Folktales of Justice: Tales of Jurisdiction', in Minow, M., Ryan, M., and Sarat, A. (eds), *Narrative, Violence and the Law: The Essays of Robert Cover*, Ann Arbor, MI: University of Michigan Press.

Davenport, F. (1917) *European Treaties Bearing on the History of the United States and its Dependencies to 1648*, Washington, DC: Carnegie Institute of Washington.

Dorsett, S. (2002) '"Since Time Immemorial": A Story of Common Law Jurisdiction, Native Title and the *Case of Tanistry*', *Melbourne University Law Review* 26: 32–59.

Douzinas, C. (2007) *Human Rights and Empire: The Political Philosophy of Cosmopolitanism*, London: Taylor & Francis.

Goodrich, P. (2008) 'Visive Powers: Colours, Trees and Genres of Jurisdiction', *Law and Humanities* 2: 213–231.

Heaney, S. (2002) *Finders Keepers: Selected Prose 1971–2001*, London: Faber & Faber.

Kantorowicz, E. (1957) *The King's Two Bodies: A Study in Mediaeval Political Theology*, Chichester: Princeton University Press.

Orford, A. (2011) *International Authority and the Responsibility to Protect*, Cambridge: Cambridge University Press.

Rush, P. (1997) 'An Altered Jurisdiction: Corporeal Traces of Law', *Griffith Law Review* 6: 144–168.

Tuck, R. (1979) *Natural Rights Theories: Their Origin and Development*, Cambridge: Cambridge University Press.

Chapter 2

Forms of jurisdiction

In this chapter, we start our consideration of jurisdiction by setting out a number of key ideas about jurisdiction. We present jurisdiction as a practice and conduct of law and as a distinct form of critical engagement with law. These ideas will reappear throughout the book.

Who speaks and who listens? Forms of jurisdictional engagement

In jurisdiction might be found questions of the inauguration or creation of law and its articulation – its value and validity. It is with these concerns, and with the representation of the orders of law that are engendered through jurisdiction, that this book engages. The critical concern addressed in this book is the quality of the engagement of lawful relations. In other words, how we come to belong to law, and the quality of that belonging. In this chapter, therefore, we consider four aspects of jurisdiction which give rise to our critical approach to jurisdiction.

Authority and authorisation

That law and jurisdiction are concerned with authority is a truism in Western legal orders. While authority can be understood in many ways according to different political and jurisprudential traditions, it has broadly been concerned with the explanation of the legitimate means of affiliation and subordination. For the political thinker, Hannah Arendt, authority can be contrasted with reason and with power. Reason, argues Arendt, is concerned with persuasion between equals, force is concerned with domination. Authority gives people reasons to submit – perhaps without servility (Arendt 1961). Much political thought, especially as it crosses into law, is concerned with justifying authority. The Western tradition has developed many accounts of the authority of God, reason, the state, the people and custom. For example, the authority of the sovereign territorial state to subject people to government is today frequently justified by popular sovereignty and consent, while the English common law tradition has linked questions of authority to those of the inheritance and transmission of customary laws.

How relations between jurisdiction and authority are understood and disputed will depend on how you understand authority (and the political and legal theory of authority) and on how you understand jurisdiction. Within jurisprudence, questions of authority are often concerned with establishing legitimate sources of law and argument (Raz 2009; Finnis 2011). While this is a proper question for jurisprudence – 'How do we understand legal authority?' – the way in which the question is addressed can obscure that such questions are also ones of jurisdiction. Within jurisprudence we often reduce the matter of authority to one of source. Legal doctrine further reduces jurisdiction to a matter of rules of law.

It is implicit in our brief formulation of jurisdiction in Chapter 1, however, that if jurisdiction inaugurates the law it must also in some sense precede it. This raises a number of conceptual and institutional questions about the nature and sources of authority. In particular, the idea that jurisdiction inaugurates law brings with it subsequent questions of transmission – how authority gets passed from one place to another – and the sense that each jurisdiction works as its own source of authority.

The relationship between jurisdiction and questions of authority has a long and complex history. For Western legal idioms, some of the most important historical formulations of this relationship are found in medieval law. There the language of jurisdiction was used to draw distinctions between *auctoritas* and *potestas* (authority and power) and in a complex way between *imperium* and *dominium* (Berman 1983: 114–115). The concepts of authority and power have been inherited in various ways. For example, the language of *potestas* is associated with political power and that of *auctoritas* with legal authority or jurisdiction. So one of the distinctive formulations of sovereignty is the joining of those two in the formation of the modern state, a matter to which we return in Chapter 3. *Imperium* might be thought of as power without limit, while *dominium* is a delegated power.

Part of the critical approach to law has involved a questioning of the authority of laws, of state law and even of law in general. One aim of this book is to show that the language and work of jurisdiction is more complex than its current usage in legal thought and practice suggests. It is necessary to pay close attention to the language of authority and of legal authority in order to criticise law effectively. It is also necessary to pay attention to the ways in which jurisdiction represents or authorises law. Fail to do this and you run the risk of producing accounts of authority that do not touch the institutional life of law or that miss the ways in which authority is exercised.

Representation

If we say that jurisdiction authorises law, the question which follows is what is being authorised? In modern law, we split this question between authority and authorisation. When we think of the exercise of a jurisdiction, we need to think about both the author and that which is being authorised. The author is the person who speaks (decides, determines, judges) the law (the institutional question). What is authorised is the law – but if we think of law simply as 'rules' then we miss much of the institutional existence of law.

Questions of authority and representation can be posed in many different ways in politics and law. The language of author and authorisation, representative and representation, and even person and personation, all gain their modern currency in 17th-century political and legal thought. The issue for the philosopher Thomas Hobbes was that of the political representation of the sovereign (Hobbes 1968: Pt 1, ch 16, 217–222). Hobbes' discussion combines a concern with the legal ordering of authority, a jurisdictional matter for us, and the representative form of authority (the outward appearance or the visible form of the sovereign). We are used to the idea of representation in terms of accounts of political authority, for example the theory of representative government and political representatives, but we can also think of law in those terms as well. So in terms of the authorisation of legal authority, the office of the legal representative and the characterisation of lawful relations can be understood in terms of persons and personality. However, when we characterise lawful relations in terms of persons and personalities, we often do not pay a lot of attention to the actual work of representation. A significant concern in this book is to link the work of jurisdiction to that of representation.

Representation gives us the visual form of law. Although we do not really think this way today, there is, clearly, a strong tradition of the representation of the authority of law. In early modern law (canon law or common law) there were rival accounts of how authority was derived and how it was understood. Broadly speaking, for canon law, for example, authority was represented by the Western Church or the institution of the Papacy (Goodrich 2008). The common law came to see itself as sourced in, and representative of, tradition 'time out of mind' (Pocock 1987) as exercised through the central courts of the common law. Jurisdiction continues to be fundamentally linked to both representation and institution – to the author of the law and the law which they authorise. Take a visual example: the coronation chair. For the last 700 years, almost all British sovereigns have been crowned on the chair. The chair, therefore, is a visible representation of the investiture of the monarch. When seated in the chair, the monarch is anointed and so a jurisdiction (crown authority) is inaugurated. Thinking jurisdictionally might lead us to ask questions of this inauguration such as 'Who is the author?' and 'What is being authorised?'.

A different kind of visible representation might be a text such as the preamble to a constitution. As examples, both the constitutions of the United States and South Africa inaugurate jurisdictions in the sense of inaugurating nations, but they also provide us with images of the nation. They tell us why the nation is coming into being, who is authorising its inauguration (the author question) and on what it is to be founded (what is being authorised). The US Constitution is a direct rejection of the previous tyrannies of the English monarchy. It tells us specifically that it is being brought into being 'in order to form a more perfect Union, establish Justice, ensure domestic Tranquility, provide for the common defence, promote the general Welfare and secure the Blessings of Liberty to ourselves and our Posterity'. The mechanism is by 'ordaining and establishing this Constitution for the United States of America'. One could say that 'ordain' is the jurisdictional word here. The author, as most will know, is 'we the people'. In a similar, but more modern vein, the South African Constitution 'recognises the injustices of their past, honour[s] those who suffered for justice and freedom in our land, respect[s] those who have worked to build and develop our country and believe that South Africa belongs to all those who live in it, united in our diversity'. The jurisdictional term is 'adopted' and the jurisdiction is authored by 'We, the people of South Africa'.

From these examples, we can see that when we are thinking about representation we should not restrict questions of representation simply to visual images, we need to hold on to the sense that jurisdiction is engaged in a range of representational practices. In this book, representation is expressed or used as much through the language of theatre as the language of art. So we can think of representation as being about the staging and performance of law – it is a production which includes sets (visual) and actors (dialogue). Representation is an activity rather than simply an image.

Jurisdiction represents the authority of law. In this book, we do not treat questions of authority as questions only of abstract will or rules, but as questions of representation. While it is tempting to describe all representation in law as jurisdictional, to do so runs the risk of losing the particular subject matter of jurisdiction in the common law tradition. While we make a considerable use of the language of representation, we tend to draw it back to questions of legal form and ordering. When we talk about jurisdiction we do not consider all the speech of law, but that speech which gives distinctive form to law and to its modes of authorisation. While we talk here about 'form', when we later discuss our critical approach it will be clear that we see form and content as being quite closely aligned in the practices of jurisdiction.

Jurisdiction as a technology of law and the technologies of jurisdiction

If we think of jurisdiction as an activity or practice, the question of representation becomes linked to that of the technologies of law. In other words, we need to think about the devices through which representation is enacted. A technology might be thought of as a practice, device, technique or organisational strategy. So, a technology or device is something that is designed to, or is capable of, authorising, changing or altering lawful relations. We discuss the concept of technology, and why jurisdiction should be considered as a craft, in some detail in Chapter 4. Suffice it to say here that thinking about jurisdiction as a technology enables us to understand how jurisdiction works in law. It helps us to work out how to do things with law. Thought of in this way, jurisdiction is a practical and technical activity. It is, however, a specific kind of technical activity. As a technology, jurisdiction produces legal meaning. It is a jurisprudence.

The most obvious example of a technology of jurisdiction is the establishment of a process or mechanism for administering justice. As jurisdiction is a power to speak the law, then the technology (device) though which this occurs is the court or even an administrative tribunal. The structures of the administration of justice can tell us much about how we represent or order the law. For example, we might want to think both about which court we commence an action in, and why we commence it in that place. A consideration of why family law is generally administered by a different tribunal to commercial law tells us something about how we represent relations of authority and lawful relations. Court business has always been split, not just between different common law courts but, as we shall see, between different jurisdictions and their courts. These divisions have changed over time, so that we now procedurally order business differently to say 200 years ago. However, our current divisions can tell us much not just about how we want to order court business as a matter of practicality, but also about the relative importance of different matters to the law. They also represent what belongs to law and the ordering of lawful relations. Thus, in considering this, we are interested not only in procedural formalities, but in the practice or exercise of jurisdiction through an apparatus such as the court system.

However, while the courts are the most obvious technology, there are others. In Chapter 4 we discuss a number of other useful technologies: writing, mapping and the practices of precedent and categorisation. All of these are technologies that give form to jurisdiction. A simple example, and one to which we will return, is the writing of a statement of claim. The act of writing inaugurates the jurisdiction of the law (and of a particular court) and brings a person to law. It requires a person to appear before a court and be subject to the judgment of that court. In Peter Rush's terms, the statement of claim gives the court the power and authority to speak in the name of the law (Rush 1997). We have chosen these technologies because they have a long association with the law, and with the common law in particular.

Writing both inaugurates law, as in the example above, and gives shape to the law, for example through law reporting. Mapping, an allied technology, allows the transmission of law across space and time. Mapping is one of the easiest technologies of jurisdiction to understand because it produces a visible representation of one specific mode of jurisdiction – territorial jurisdiction. On a map one can see the spatial extent and limits of the national law. Categories, on the other hand, create domains of legal knowledge. Why is something thought of as contract law, rather than tort law? In doctrinal terms, we often spend time defending the boundaries of legal areas – such as not allowing parts of equity law to eviscerate particular common law doctrines. A simple example might be the potential effect of the doctrine of equitable estoppel on contract law and the doctrine of consideration. Ordering legal knowledge is a jurisdictional practice. We locate, then, jurisdiction in the languages of authority and power and in the practices of representation as enacted through the technologies and devices of law.

Jurisdiction engages lawful relations

In the above sections we have begun to use the language of 'belonging to law' or of jurisdiction 'engaging lawful relations'. Jurisdiction inaugurates law. Thus, it brings law into being. But if jurisdiction inaugurates law, the question which must be asked is 'How and how much law'? What belongs to law, or becomes the subject of law? These questions address the shape or form of law. Jurisdiction inaugurates law, but it also delimits law – it provides the boundaries of law. It establishes and represents the ambit of lawful relations. Here, lawful simply refers to the idea of belonging to law.

By paying attention to jurisdiction rather than legal doctrine we are moving consideration from that legal doctrine to jurisprudence. Legal doctrine attends to the formalisation of legal knowledge. So in civil law, legal doctrine might be about the ordering of an area of law. In the common law, legal doctrine might concern the formalisation of legal argument (for example, by setting out the rules of formation and breach of contract). When we think about legal doctrine we do not think much about jurisdiction – if only because we largely assume jurisdiction. However, if we want to think about jurisdiction as a practice, we need to shift our attention to forms of practical reason or jurisprudence. We take jurisprudence here as a way of thinking with law. As an example, common law doctrine is concerned with the rules of contract formation or whether marriage is a contract or something else. Practical reasoning, on the other hand, is not concerned with the formal elaboration of rules, it is concerned with the judgment and address of forms of law. Is this a good means of achieving a result and is it a good result? To say this is to tie us into a particular tradition of jurisprudence. We discuss this further at the end of this chapter. The idea of belonging to law is one of the most important matters we consider in this book. What is important is not just whether something or someone belongs to law. Rather, it is the quality of belonging to law which matters.

Office of the jurist and legal doctrine

We have just offered a topical account of jurisdiction shaped around jurisdiction as a practice or form of conduct. Before we can develop a specific critical approach, we need to relate our account of jurisdiction to doctrinal approaches to legal writing and the role of the jurist as an authoritative commentator on the law. As we will see, the office of the jurist engages both doctrinal and critical thinking. What the jurist – either doctrinal or critical – does is to engage the authority of law and the institutional life of law.

Doctrinal thinking might be taken as the central mode of the organisation of legal thought. It is associated both with forms of legal science – the systematic organisation of legal materials according to a principle of reason – and with 'black letter' law, the practical organisation of legal materials for the purpose of legal practice. Legal doctrine as the systematic organisation of legal thought is closely associated with the work of the university and traditions of legal scholarship. Historically, it has been associated with the dogmatic ordering – or official teaching – of law. Doctrinal scholarship, then, gives us an account of law shaped to represent the authority of law. Critical thinking, by contrast, is turned towards the difficulties of law and, for us here, the difficulties relating to the authority and authorisation of law.

Since the 19th century, analytical legal theory has sought to distinguish between law as it is and law as it ought to be (Bentham 1823; Austin 1832; Hart 1958). This is a useful distinction for policymakers but tends to obscure the work of legal thought and legal interpretation because it says nothing about the practices of legal writing involved in representing what law is, or about the practices involved in being critical. This is so for two reasons. The first is institutional. Legal thought – and critical legal thought – relates to the practice of institutions. In many ways it is difficult to think of legal institutions without thinking about jurisdiction. The second reason is more prosaic. Legal theory has been more interested in testing concept formation than in thinking about the institutional forms of life.

Posing jurisdiction in terms of the institutional life of law also draws out the ways in which jurisdictional thinking is associated with the office of the jurist and jurisprudent. Office might loosely be understood as an institutional ordering of duties, relationships and responsibilities (Condren 2006: 66–89). In contemporary times we are used to thinking of office in terms of an institutional occupation such as that of the Lord Chancellor, a judge or the Secretary General of the United Nations. We might also think of a range of other offices such as jurist, scholar or even poet (Heaney 1995). Traditionally, the office of the jurist has been concerned with articulating law – naming, classifying and commenting on law. This is one way in which law is authorised. Critical approaches to law also continue this work of authorisation – albeit in ways that very often question the authority of law or even the possibility of a properly authorised law. In order to illustrate this, here we make brief mention of five jurists who, through doctrine or criticism, who address some important concerns of jurisdiction.

Azo of Bologna (1150–1230) was one of the school of glossators who gave conceptual form to Roman law in the 12th century. For us, his importance as jurist was that he developed the Roman law forms of *jurisdictio* and *imperium* into an early account of sovereign authority. For Roman lawyers, *jurisdictio* was a term that links authority to act to an office, role, or position. So a jurisdiction could be understood in terms of the conditions under which an authority to act exists – say an authority to transfer possession or to appoint guardians or to assign judges to litigants. *Jurisdictio* was often used in close relation to *imperium* or *dominium* (power, possession, control). The 11th-century jurists or glossators set about re-organising Roman law categories for new purposes. Azo linked *jurisdictio* and *imperium* in a way that has given us an important formulation that links jurisdiction to political power. He did so by making *imperium* a part of a larger scheme of jurisdiction. In so doing, Azo gave us a conceptual scheme that frames jurisdiction in terms of the power to pronounce judgment and to establish justice. He also framed the princes' right to rule and legislate in terms of a power to adjudicate. In doing this, Azo began the task of distinguishing different forms of authority and power to rule and to judge. Azo did not give us the first formulation of these questions, but he gave them an enduring legal form. By the 15th century these concerns were taken up into the consideration of sovereignty, a matter we return to in Chapter 2.

Mathew Hale (1609–1676) was a judge of the Court of Common Pleas and Chief Justice of the Court of King's Bench. His *History of the Common Law* published in 1713 (Hale 1971) is a classic example of a law treatise from the period. The 18th century saw the emergence of some of the first attempts to organise and systematise the knowledge of law. Much of Hale's work is concerned with explaining and describing various jurisdictions and their relationships. Importantly, Hale undertook to describe the relationship between the common law and its 'rivals', for example ecclesiastical law and the law merchant, through the lens of jurisdiction. He re-framed the relations between them through an overall framework in which the common law emerged as the dominant jurisdiction in England. Hale's work reminds us that even in an era in which jurists were looking to systematise the common law, jurisdictional relations both within and without the common law were still key to any understanding of the English legal system.

The work of the jurist Justice Oliver Wendell Holmes (1841–1935) has had a lasting influence on the development of American common law and legal theory. At first glance, his work on tort law does not look like offering a jurisdictional account of law. However, categories of law, like tort law, can be thought of as technologies of jurisdiction in the sense that they create a jurisdictional domain. In the first half of the 19th century, there was no recognisable category of tort law. Rather, what came to constitute tort law existed through a number of forms of action – trespass, trespass on the case and trover for example. Jurisdiction to litigate what we now think of as tort was acquired by coming within one of these writs. As a domain (a jurisdiction) of law this area had little coherent substantive content (in fact, even the term 'substantive' was not really in use). With the demise of the writs, Holmes was instrumental in transforming a collection of actions into the modern American conception of tort law. As early as 1873, in his essay 'The Theory of Torts' Holmes fashioned tort law as a jurisdictional domain which had 'liability for negligence' at its centre (Grey 2001). We discuss the idea of categories of law as jurisdictions in Chapter 3.

Perhaps the work of jurists who write on jurisdiction with which we are most familiar is that of the private international lawyers, and particularly those who write on conflicts of law. An example of an influential text in this area is Dicey's *The Conflict of Laws* (Collins *et al* 2010). In these accounts we can see that the most common formulation of jurisdiction in modern law – one in which jurisdiction itself is a facet of sovereignty – is reduced to a descriptive fact. A key task is to resolve whose jurisdiction is to prevail in situations where there is a choice of law or it is unclear which of several bodies of law (the law of Singapore, the law of the United States or the law of Australia) will be determinative.

Our final example we take from Robert Cover (1943–1986), a civil rights activist and professor of law in the United States at Yale University. As a jurisdictional writer, Robert Cover's work is more concerned with jurisprudence, with the practical form and reasoning of law, than with legal science or legal doctrine (Cover 1993a, 1993b, 1993c). Jurisdiction, for Robert Cover, is the work of the creation and authorisation of normative worlds and of the authorisation of institutions capable of judging and of projecting new meaning into the future – 'of bridging the world that is' and the projections of alternative 'worlds-that-might-be' (Cover 1993a: 176). Robert Cover made this observation in the course of a discussion of the possibilities of the establishment of the jurisdiction of the war crimes tribunals at Nuremberg in 1946. However, he was also interested in the many ways in which speaking 'truth to power' can be given jurisdictional form. For Cover, the 'International War Crimes Tribunal' established by the philosophers and public intellectuals Bertrand Russell and Jean Paul Sartre counted as one such jurisdiction (Duffett 1968). Russell and Sartre self-consciously linked their tribunal to the 'revolutionary' jurisdictions established by the American and French revolutionaries of the 18th century, and the socialist revolutionaries of the 19th and 20th centuries (Cover 1993a: 198–201).

Being critical

This book is part of a series of critical approaches to law. We offer here a brief explanation of our approach to jurisdiction as a way of thinking about law and as a way of thinking with law. This we take as one of the central concerns of jurisprudence (and the office of jurisprudent). The relationships between jurisprudence (legal theory) and accounts of jurisdiction are varied. Each tradition and epoch of jurisprudence develops its own understanding of jurisdiction and its associated topics. The understanding of jurisdiction and the modes of the authorisation of law are shaped by the sorts of jurisprudential commitments that we make in the study and practice of law. In this book, we have chosen to concentrate of the technical and material forms of jurisdictional practice. We have done so in order to make visible a way of addressing questions of law through jurisdiction. This approach is not presented as a full theory of law but rather it is an orientation to law that marks certain forms of conduct and commitment to lawful relations. In this section, we explain what this means and how our approach might relate to broader critical traditions of jurisprudence. The critical approach to law taken in this book does not look for ways and means of transcending or escaping law but seeks to deepen and expand the ways of engaging with law. While our political concern lies with questions of injustice, our legal concern lies with the formation of lawful relations. Our ethical and jurisprudential concern rests with the acknowledgement of human relations and the humanising of lawful relations. We join institutional forms of jurisdictional practice or craft to those of authority, dignity, office and role – and only then to that of justiciability and justice.

Critical approaches to law are varied and frequently offer competing accounts of what is wrong with law and what is required by way of remedy or transformation. For some, being critical registers a concern with the maintenance or restoration of the legal order. Here, for example, might be found the reformulations of the traditional common law in legal judgments (Bingham 2010). The concern lies with justice or with other legal values that are inherent or immanent in the legal order. A second form of critical encounter is more concerned with the gap between law and justice and the reform of law towards an external measure of justice. This in a sense is the approach of the critic as legal reformer and policy expert. The horizons of justice for such projects have been varied, but in an era of political equality and human rights our critical languages are shaped by the claims of liberty, equality, dignity and community. A third form of engagement is more obviously critical. Law does not need reforming but transforming and re-founding (Habermas 1996; Dworkin 1986). However, for many critics, this activity produces a complex and often fraught relation with law. As critics, we struggle with the need to maintain law as an effective instrument of government and change, but at the same time we need to engage with the critical work of the transformation of law. One prevalent critical response to this has been to seek to join these two concerns and so to perfect the law in an ideal form.

Douzinas and Geary characterise the search for an ideal form of law in terms of the renewal of law and the demand for justice. Since the 18th century, they argue, modern critique has attempted to subject law to forms of critical reason. Immanuel Kant, and exponents of the Kantian tradition, have sought the logical conditions of transcendent reason: it is reason that gives us the form and limit of thought, including practical and moral thought. We are to criticise, but within the limits of reason alone (Douzinas and Geary 2005: 36–38). For example, in a Kantian account, human rights could be viewed as an expression of universal value capable of being formulated in ways that treat humans as ends in themselves and not only means. Critical inquiry would then be directed to the investigation of the conditions of the universal expression of human value.

Another critical tradition, associated with Georg Hegel and Karl Marx, has turned reason to the task of revealing the true forms of the freedom of human, social and economic relations. Here the critic is not setting the form and limits of reason but seeking the true realisation of human relations. The Marxist traditions have attended both to the investigation of the economic forces and relations of the production of social relations and to the ways in which relations of power have alienated humans from their labour and have turned social relations into objects of exchange. Jurisprudents within this tradition have also sought to expose and realise the promise of emancipatory justice (Bloch 1987; Kochi 2010). Critical thinking in this context is directed toward exposing false forms of human relations and toward marking the conditions of the realisation of human freedom. So, for example, contemporary forms of human rights could be criticised for the way in which they represent the values and freedom of First World property holders as universal and beyond dispute. But human rights might also be capable of reformulation as part of an emancipatory claim for genuine universality.

While we are sympathetic to traditions of critique, especially those framed in terms of the investigation of the material forms of freedom, we take a rather more restrained approach to engaging lawful relations. In this book, we offer an approach to law that pays attention to what it might mean to think with jurisdiction. If relations of power can still be addressed as concerns of legality and lawful relations, it is important to be able to address the technical forms such concerns take. We opened this chapter by ordering jurisdiction around the concerns of authority, forms of representation, technology and the articulation of lawful relations. Our sense of the importance of jurisdiction is shaped around the practical concern that jurisdiction is a mode and manner of instituting forms of conduct of life before the law. In this book, we try to hold closely to the practical means of jurisdiction in order to investigate its resources. We are used to thinking of jurisdiction as a part of procedure or administrative law, but doctrinal lawyers and critics alike spend very little time thinking about what it is that the technologies and techniques of jurisdiction make available to legal thought and legal practice. For us, it is of central importance to attend to the ways jurisdiction as a technology is capable of representing and carrying meaning about lawful conduct. Without this attention there is a risk that any critical approach to law will simply miss the complex ways in which relations between authority and modes of authorisation create and address lawful relations and the practical conditions of legal existence. It is also important to analyse the ways in which the modes and manner of the exercise of jurisdiction (as power) are put to use.

In her famous work on the humane killing of animals in abattoirs, Temple Grandin describes how she studied the whole process of the slaughter from the point of view of the animal (Grandin and Johnson 2005). By taking the viewpoint of the animal, she argued, she was able to minimise the trauma and suffering caused to it. Ian Hacking shows some of the ways in which following such a critical 'process' might give pause for thought. The upshot of this research is that we can now understand how cattle or pigs might be terrified by a shadow or shape or light. From this might be garnered a number of insights. One of these is that there are more 'efficient' and 'humane' ways of killing animals in abattoirs. The definition of humane killing of cattle in US abattoirs still allows for the use of electric prods in 25% of cases in order to drive cattle to slaughter. This, as Ian Hacking notes, can give us pause for thought (Hacking 2008: 150). His analysis shows a procedure which allows us to engage in a form of analysis that results in the alleviation of suffering. At the same time, however, it makes killing animals more effective.

Many of the same considerations might be made in thinking about the limits of jurisdictional thought as a concern of administration or procedure. Thinking with jurisdiction invites more concern with means than with ultimate ends.

The critical approach to jurisdiction taken up in this book then is threefold. First, we develop jurisdiction as a way of working with law as a medium of the creation, representation and disposition of lawful relations. Second, we re-describe a number of accounts of law in order to make them amenable to analysis as questions of the authority of law and the modes of authorisation of law. This gives us a way to address the style and the technical forms of living with the law. Stated in this way our approach to jurisdiction is not necessarily critical except in the sense that it invokes an ethic of responsibility for the forms that law takes on. We discuss this further later in the chapter. Finally, our approach to jurisdiction takes up the possibilities of imagining and creating new jurisdictions and new forms of legal relation. For example, what forms of jurisdiction might be needed to re-describe our relationship to the land for the purposes of tackling climate change or for reasons of achieving ecological justice? Or, perhaps, what jurisdictional forms would be appropriate for bringing non-indigenous laws more properly into relation with indigenous laws and jurisprudence?

Earlier in the chapter, we briefly discussed the idea that jurisdiction engages lawful relations. One of the matters which follows on from this is that of the extent to which we belong to law and the equality of that belonging. This directly raises the question of how deeply law institutes life. For some this could be viewed as a strong claim. Alain Supiot, for example, encapsulates this claim in terms of our transformation into a *homo juridicus* (Supiot 2007). The law for Supiot brings us from a biological existence into legal being. In other words, the law gives structure to our social existence. The question is how deeply that structure lies. The Christian religious traditions have given us a deep structure that orders both our conscience and our social form – the twin characteristics of the legal subject. How we view the legal subject has always been a matter of dispute. On one side, we talk about law instituting life. Jurists like Supiot and Legendre insist that all of our social or symbolic existence should be thought of in terms of law, so that, for example, to remove or deny legal personality is to remove or deny existence (Legendre 1997). An example might be the stateless asylum seeker, who, once legal personality has been removed, is beyond the protection and limits of law. On the other side, there are those who see law as a technical device that operates without creating deep social relations. In this account what is important about law is that it is a technical means to achieve social effects, rather than a device to create all of social existence. One example could be that in one tradition we could think of law as creating a profound distinction between sacred space (religion) and profane market place (trade) or we could see law as simply creating a boundary between two spaces, rather than creating what is sacred or profane (Thomas 2004). Yifat Hachamovitch elaborates the point of affiliation by stating:

> There is no human bone that does not also support a dogma, no mouth through which the law does not speak , no kiss that does not also enfeoff. The body is a medieval compilation which we have inherited alongside the *Corpus Juris* and the barbarian codes. It is a Roman institution hammered together with Christian nails. From the 11th to the 13th centuries it is assembled and dissembled by medieval lawyers, alongside the pages of the legal text; it is compiled along with the political and juridical concept of the Justinian compilation, it accumulates a history through the sedimentation of legal signs.
>
> (Hachamovitch 1990: 187)

Others will view the inheritance of law only in terms of technique.

Part of the investigation of this book then is to consider how much meaning law can carry. In accounts that make law central to life we could think of law as instituting the forms of life that are available to us as human and legal subjects. Jurisdictional thinking draws attention to the styles of becoming human and social – it gives us our forms of responsibility and of relationship. It also gives us our place in the world or, better, our patterns of engaging or relating with the world. If jurisdiction, as we will argue, opens the space of law by giving us the extent of law, how is this to be understood? In modern times, the extent or scope of jurisdiction has often been framed in terms of space – most commonly in the form of territorial sovereignty, but jurisdiction does not need to be linked to territory or to land. It can operate through a number of modes – for example attaching to a person's status (being a minor, a soldier or a refugee, for instance) or activities (often governed by modern administrative tribunals).

In summation, our critical approach to law and to approaching law through jurisdiction is less concerned with formal critique than with the modes and manner of coming into law and with the ways in which we live with law. Questions of jurisdiction turn our attention to the institution, judgment, and address of law. However, we do not subject jurisdictional arrangements to the critical tribunal of reason or history. Approaching law through jurisdictional thought and practice draws out the ways in which we engage law through its forms of authorisation and representation, its technologies and techniques, and its modes of address. We are, of course, still very much concerned with what such activities do to human lives. One consequence and limit of thinking with jurisdiction is that the certain practices and ways of understanding law are given prominence over other forms of legal engagement. Jurisdiction as a mode of authorising law pays considerable attention to questions of authority and legality. It worries rather less about justice and the justification of lawful relations. For some this will be a weakness. Here we accept it as a limit of our approach. In the final section of this chapter we consider some of the forms of responsibility that might be appropriate to approaches to law taken through jurisdiction.

Why do we use history?

In discussing jurisdiction we turn frequently to history. Why in a work of jurisprudence is history a privileged resource? First, the broadest claim of our jurisprudence is that our conception of law is itself historical. The broadest understanding of law – and of the institutional life of law – is historical. This understanding of law operates on two registers. At one level, it is a claim that law, in particular the common law tradition, is strongly shaped by institutional practices. One example might be property law. While we can teach and learn property law as a series of transactions, the answer to why something works the way it does can often only be answered by explaining the history of the particular property institution at issue. Why does the fee tail limit the class of descendants? Why is a lease classified as a chattel real? (Murphy *et al* 2004).

Likewise, jurisdictional thought is strongly shaped by the history of legal institutions and legal thought. At various parts in this book we discuss the histories of some of the many jurisdictions which existed alongside the common law in the pre-modern (and into the early modern) period. Today, we have largely forgotten that the common law was once one of hundreds of jurisdictions across England, each with its own institutional history and logic. The common law developed its own internal ways of relating to these other domains of legal knowledge. Similarly, across the empire the common law encountered other, foreign, jurisdictions, and developed ways of relating to these. These institutional practices still underpin much of modern common law thinking and how we think now about questions of law and of legal order. As a practical matter, for example, one can see these histories in modern rules on conflicts of laws. One particular institution that is of relevance here is the modern territorial state and corresponding territorial jurisdiction. The emergence of this institution, and in particular the simultaneous loss of the alternative, non-common law, jurisdictions had a profound effect on how we understand jurisdiction now. Whereas once we understood jurisdiction as attaching to bodies of law (for example common law, ecclesiastical law or the law of the forest), now we understand it as being about technical matters such as selection of forum. How this came to be our modern approach to jurisdiction is an important story and one which is crucial to thinking about how jurisdiction functions both within and without the state. It allows us to address the variety and significance of legal form.

The second reason for thinking about jurisdiction in historical terms follows on from the first, but is largely practical. Commentary on modern law, including critical commentary, is dominated by a particular structure and analytical form. There is a very strong temptation to view law as a system and to think of system as a coherent whole. In a similar manner, accounts of legal interpretation adopt 'formal' or 'formalist' accounts of interpretation and adjudication. In this book, we do not draw a distinction between 'formal' and 'informal' accounts of law or interpretation. A strong argument presented in this book is that jurisdictional practice should indeed be viewed as a practice – a way of doing things rather than a completed or ideal form. The forms or structures through which we think of 'the legal system' are relatively recent and should not be thought of as the only way in which law can be structured. Reference to historical materials can show us different institutional practices and provide different ways in which we can think about jurisdictional practices and arrangements. In part then this concern is therapeutic. It also helps with the development of a wider range of resources and repertoires of jurisdictional argument than can be seen from our modern jurisdictional arrangements. These repertoires of argument can help us to think in other ways about current issues of law – such as thinking about the legal organisation of euthanasia. We work through some examples in Chapters 4 and 5. The third reason for thinking about jurisdiction in historical terms is to bring out the sense of prudence and of deliberation that is available in contemporary jurisprudences of jurisdiction. The language of prudence and of critical jurisprudence is not one that is easy to keep in focus. Attending to the historical forms of jurisdiction allows for a more nuanced consideration of jurisprudence. By setting the language of prudence within the history of the repertoires of jurisdictional practice, we also set our critical approach to law in place.

Ethic of responsibility

Within Western idioms of jurisprudence our understanding of law and jurisdiction is still very much shaped by an understanding of a sovereign who commands and governs. Part of the concern of this book is to investigate the ways in which jurisdictional practices are not simply concerned with (legitimate) forms of subordination but also establish forms of legal community and lawful conduct (Young 2011). This is one of the central concerns of a critical jurisprudence of jurisdiction. In the final part of this chapter we consider an ethic of responsibility appropriate to thinking through the idioms of jurisdiction. A jurisprudence of jurisdiction allows us to take responsibility for a range of practices of authority, representation, and conduct. Here we link an ethic of responsibility to the office of the jurisprudent and a concern for maintaining a connection between lawful and human relations. This orientation does not, we think, provide an effective resource for all critical thought about law. It does, however, give a significant shape to critical jurisprudence.

The formulation of an ethic of responsibility of jurisdiction also raises questions about the forms of responsibility appropriate to the office of university jurist. For better and worse the idioms of the Western legal tradition engage with the shape and limits of responsibility. Our critical approach to jurisdiction and to law through jurisdiction is to hold as closely as possible to jurisdictional thinking and practice. This involves considering, on the one hand, the ways in which such practices bring with them forms of responsibility and, on the other, to consider the commitments that other forms of critical engagement suggest by way of jurisdictional engagement. Perhaps even more so than questions of form, questions of responsibility for law invite dispute and confusion. So we will be as specific as possible with our first introduction to what we mean by responsibility of form and then we will elaborate our argument as we pass through the book. The critical approach we are taking to jurisdiction and to law through jurisdiction can be labelled in terms of an ethic of responsibility.

Max Weber's famous lecture 'Politics as Vocation' presented in 1919 (Weber 1919) provides a good point of departure. Weber's lecture is concerned with the sort of character necessary for taking up and holding on to political office. For us the work of jurisdiction is the responsibility of the office of the jurist and the jurisprudent. Just as there can be no jurisprudence – no account of the practical reason of law – without an account of jurisdiction, there can be no account of jurisdiction without attending to the forms of response and responsibility it invites and makes available. Weber's starting point for his argument about office is to link office both to institutional activity and to a number of external and internal realities. The lecture is framed in terms of finding the appropriate internal qualities to meet external realities. In this lecture, and others, Weber makes this engagement speaking as a scholar rather than a moralist or political activist. His analysis – and ours – is marked by the limits that this office imposes. For Weber this limit relates to his sense of the limits of positive political economy. For us it relates to forms of conduct associated with the exercise of jurisdiction. The distinction Weber draws out is between an ethic of responsibility that addresses what is done and an ethic of conviction that is concerned with intention. The ethic of conviction is criticised by Weber for its willingness to indulge subjective predisposition (and ideology) against an ethic of office. For Weber, the responsible actor is the one who is able to engage the facts of life and the values of office in the knowledge that many actions do not add up or are incapable of adequate justification. While jurisdictional thinking is integral to law, it is not always amenable to straightforward critical or ethical evaluation.

Taking the world as one finds it might require, for example, some acknowledgement that the common law order of the world pursues incompatible ends (or pursues ends without much meaning or understanding, such as administrative efficacy and substantive justice). More importantly, for Weber the ethic of modern office is shaped around the discussion of procedures, not of ends. This identifies an important characteristic in relation to jurisdiction. If a jurisdiction is a grant of authority, or it inaugurates authority, it also gives us a legal form that takes on an existence apart from substantive issues. It does not escape the situation that there are inevitably conflicts and incompatibilities. Many of these difficulties stem from the intimate engagement of the common law with British and other imperial projects as well as with the histories and practices of dispossession of indigenous peoples. It might also be the case that the administrative and bureaucratic impetus of jurisdictional thinking is destined to defeat an engagement of laws and render substantive engagements of lawful relations meaningless from the point of view of politics (and ethics).

Weber, we think, provides an important starting point for thinking about a critical approach to law through jurisdiction. As the book proceeds our argument will develop the ethic of responsibility in a number of ways. First, and most obvious, the ethic of responsibility presented by many critics of law is not content with aligning an ethic of responsibility with the law and offices of the state. The plurality of jurisdictional forms that we investigate in this book invite consideration of a plurality of forms of responsibility. Second, it is necessary to attend to the limits of responsibility made available through forms of doctrinal and critical understanding of law. The common law brings with it its own 'responsibility practices' (Cane 2002: 4) many of which are structured around extremely limited accounts of responsibility (Veitch 2007). Talk of responsibility – and even the concept of responsibility – has a social and historical form. Finally, in occupying the office of jurisprudent we have taken as a measure (horizon of value) the acknowledgement of forms of human and lawful relationship. We treat this in part as a question of attending to the 'texture' or form of jurisdictional practice and in part a matter of orientation towards human relations.

Conclusion

In this chapter, we have given a brief account of the forms of jurisdiction and our critical approach to law through jurisdiction. In doing this we have indicated that our approach joins other traditions of critical thinking but does so in a restricted way. We are not seeking a critical engagement with the form of law as such (if there is such a form) but with particular forms of law – mostly from within the common law tradition. As the book proceeds, we deepen and elaborate the accounts of authority and authorisation of law through jurisdiction. The critical approaches shaped by the forms of prudence made available by jurisdictional practice are limited. In one respect the sense of limit is productive: it allows us to examine the repertoires of jurisdictional practice and it allows us to maintain some clarity about what can be said and done with law. It also provides a sense of a limit to critical thinking with jurisdiction. We address law, and its limitations, by taking responsibility for these forms and the lawful relations they realise.

References

Arendt, H. (1961) *Between Past and Future: Six Essays in Political Thought*, New York, NY: The Viking Press.
Austin, J. (1832) *Province of Jurisprudence Determined*, London: J Murray.
Bentham, J. (1823) *Introduction to the Principles of Morals and Legislation*, 2 vols, London: Pickering.

Berman, H. (1983) *Law and Revolution*, Cambridge, MA: Harvard University Press.

Bingham, T. (2010) *The Rule of Law*, London: Allen Lane.

Bloch, E. (1987) *Natural Law and Human Dignity*, Cambridge, MA: MIT Press.

Cane, P. (2002) *Responsibility in Law and Morality*, London: Routledge-Cavendish.

Collins, L., Briggs, A., Harris, J., McClean, J.D., McLachlan, C. and Morse, C. (eds) (2010) *Dicey, Morris and Collins: The Conflict of Laws*, 14th edn, with 4th supp, London: Sweet & Maxwell.

Condren, C. (2006) 'The *Persona* of the Philosopher and the Rhetorics of Office in Early Modern England', in Condren, C., Gaukroger, S., and Hunter, I. (eds), *The Philosopher in Early Modern Europe: The Nature of a Contested Identity*, Cambridge: Cambridge University Press.

Cover, R. (1993a) 'The Folktales of Justice: Tales of Jurisdiction', in Minow, M., Ryan, M. and Sarat, A. (eds), *Narrative, Violence, and the Law: The Essays of Robert Cover*, Ann Arbor, MI: University of Michigan Press.

Cover, R. (1993b) 'Nomos and Narrative', in Minow, M., Ryan, M. and Sarat, A. (eds), *Narrative, Violence, and the Law: The Essays of Robert Cover*, Ann Arbor, MI: University of Michigan Press.

Cover, R. (1993c) 'Violence and the Word', in Minow, M., Ryan, M. and Sarat, A. (eds), *Narrative, Violence, and the Law: The Essays of Robert Cover*, Ann Arbor, MI: University of Michigan Press.

Douzinas, C. and Geary, A. (2005) *Critical Jurisprudence*, Oxford: Hart Publishing.

Duffett, J. (ed) (1968) *Against the Crime of Silence: Proceedings of the Russell International War Crimes Tribunal*, New York, NY: O'Hare Books.

Dworkin. R. (1986) *Law's Empire*, London: Fontana.

Finnis, J. (2011) *Natural Law and Natural Rights*, 2nd edn (1st edn, 1981), Oxford: Oxford University Press.

Goodrich, P. (2008) 'Visive Powers: Colours, Trees and Genres of Jurisdiction', *Law and Humanities* 2: 213–231.

Grandin, T. and Johnson, C. (2005) *Animals in Translation: Using the Mysteries of Autism to Decode Animal Behavior*, New York, NY: Harcourt, Brace, Jovanovich.

Grey, T. (2001) 'Accidental Torts', *Vanderbilt Law Review* 54: 1225–1284.

Habermas, J. (1996) *Between Facts and Norms* (Rehg, W. trans), Cambridge: Polity Press.

Hachamovitch, Y. (1990) 'One Law on the Other', *International Journal of the Semiotics of Law* 3: 187–200.

Hacking, I. (2008) 'Deflections', in Cavell, S., Diamond, C., McDowell, J., Hacking, I. and Wolfe, C. (eds), *Philosophy and Animal Life*, New York, NY: Columbia University Press.

Hale, M. (1971) *The History of the Common Law of England, and An Analysis of the Civil Part of the Law* (Gray, C. ed), Chicago, IL: The University of Chicago Press.

Hart, H.L.A. (1958) 'Positivism and the Separation of Law and Morals', *Harvard Law Review* 71: 593–629.

Heaney, S. (1995) *The Redress of Poetry: Oxford Lectures*, London: Faber & Faber.

Hobbes, R. (1968) *Leviathan*, Harmondsworth: Penguin.

Kochi, T. (2010) *The Other's War*, London: Routledge.

Legendre, P. (1997) 'Law and the Unconscious', in Goodrich, P. (ed), *Law and the Unconscious: A Legendre Reader*, Basingstoke: Macmillan Press.

Murphy, R., Roberts, S. and Flessas, T. (2004) *Understanding Property Law*, 4th edn, London: Sweet & Maxwell.

Pocock, J.G.A. (1987) *The Ancient Constitution and the Feudal Law: A Study of English Historical Thought in the Seventeenth Century*, 2nd edn (1st edn, 1957), Cambridge: Cambridge University Press.

Raz, J. (2009) *The Authority of Law: Essays on Law and Morality*, 2nd edn, Oxford: Oxford University Press.

Rush, P. (1997) 'An Altered Jurisdiction: Corporeal Traces of Law', *Griffith Law Review* 6: 144–168.

Supiot, A. (2007) *Homo Juridicus* (Brown, S. trans), London: Verso

Thomas, Y. (2004) '*Res Religiosi:* On the Categories of Religion and Commerce in Roman Law', in Pottage, A. and Mundy, M. (eds), *Law, Anthropology, and the Constitution of the Social: Making Persons and Things*, Cambridge: Cambridge University Press.

Veitch, S. (2007) *Law and Irresponsibility: On the Legitimation of Human Suffering*, London: Routledge-Cavendish.

Weber, M. (1919) reprinted and translated in Owen, D.S., Strong, T.B. and Livingstone, R. (eds) (2004) *The Vocation Lectures*, Indianapolis, IN: Hackett Publishing.

Young, I. (2011) *Responsibility for Justice*, New York, NY: Oxford University Press.

Chapter 3

Authority and authorisation: sovereignty, territory, jurisdiction

In this chapter we draw out the ways in which the jurisdictional practice of sovereignty creates legal relations. We ask how we should understand jurisdiction as a form of authority. This chapter engages with relations between sovereignty, territory, and jurisdiction. In Chapter 2, we situate authority, and legal authority, as falling somewhere between the reason and persuasion of equals and the forceful subordination of inferiors. Authority in contemporary thinking is closely associated with legitimate reasons for subordination. In political and moral philosophy, the exercise of authority can be viewed in terms of subordination without servility (Arendt 1961; Gaita 1999).

In order to show the jurisdictional links between authority and the modes of authorisation of law, we begin this chapter with the historical and institutional forms of authority within what is now the common law tradition. It is the consideration of modes of jurisdictional thought that allow an understanding of the plurality of jurisdictional forms of authority. To show this, we return here to the jurisdictional plurality of early modern law before the rise of the modern nation state in order to examine the specific formation of the English sovereign state and to pluralise the conceptual and institutional resources of jurisdictional ordering. Such an approach shifts attention away from the sovereign state towards jurisdiction as a practice of authority and the creation of lawful relations. This is a form of argument often associated with schools of pluralism, which look at the relationship between state and non-state forms of authority (Comaroff and Comaroff 2010; Engel Merry 1988). However, we are not so much concerned with non-state activity as with the consideration of the jurisdictional representation of authority. It is with this understanding that we can address the forms of responsibility associated with jurisdictional practice. Crudely, a critical approach to jurisdiction and to law must be capable of living with the forms of jurisdictional practice through which lawful relations are articulated.

Authority

For Hannah Arendt, whose work shapes much modern thinking about
authority, authority provides a point of organisation of the conservation
and renewal of a 'beginning' (Arendt 1961). This captures something of
the way in which we understand authority in the common law tradition as
engaging a relation between past, present and future. In the context of
thinking about sovereignty and jurisdiction, attending to authority
allows for a point of engagement with the mode and manner of binding
a law. A jurisdiction, as common legal formulations suggest, is a 'power
(*potestas*) to decide' but we also consider jurisdiction in terms of
authority. Joining and holding apart these aspects of jurisdiction gives us
some sense of the repertoires of jurisdiction. Linking authority and jurisdiction also brings out the idiomatic quality of jurisdiction. Questions of
authority and authorisation draw attention to who speaks and who hears
or listens in matters of jurisdiction. Western legal idioms tend to imagine
that it is the sovereign of the sovereign territorial states who speaks and
the citizen or subject who listens, but this need not be the case. There are,
as suggested in Chapter 1, two great narratives of jurisdiction and
authority within the Western legal traditions: the spiritual and temporal
authority of Church and state and their attendant jurisdictions of conscience and civility. Jurisdictions of conscience are addressed in their
modern form in Chapters 4 and 5. In this chapter, we begin our consideration of the ways in which the practices of jurisdiction authorise
law. We treat this here in terms of the representation of authority and
of lawful relations.

The Roman term *auctoritas* relates to the prestige or influence of a
person. It is associated in various ways with founding and augmentation.
In political terms, authority was associated with the authority of the
senate and was in different ways contrasted with *potestas* or *imperium*
(power) which was held by the magistrate or the people. It encapsulated
the ability to give advice or bind another. So, for example, in the 12th and
13th centuries the papacy invoked (divine) *auctoritas* as superior to
temporal (secular) power in order to exercise control (authority) over
emperors, kings and princes in Europe.

For some, this way of framing authority and jurisdiction will direct
attention straight away to 'constitutional' thinking – that is to the sorts
of public law jurisprudence that are concerned with the creation of
political orders and their government. This is an important genre of
jurisprudential thought that has been developed over the last 400 years.
Here, however, we wish to focus more on those forms of jurisdictional

authority that establish forms of legal order. This has two elements. The first involves the consideration of the ceremonial or material forms of law that mark the existence of legal institutions and give shape to lawful relations. The second concerns the institutional forms of the authorisation of law.

The material or ceremonial aspect of law draws attention to the practice of law. One example of this, discussed later, can be seen in the way authority is conferred on the monarch and the way the monarch confers authority on others. The English monarch receives his or her authority through the act of investiture, the swearing of oaths of allegiance, and institutional ceremony – such as the opening of Parliament. Such examples point not just to the fact of authority, but to the idea that authority always has to be authorised – by someone and through some institutional practice of law. They are modes of authorisation – ways in which authority is created and represented. Historically, an office holder would use a seal on documents as a symbol of his authority. A seal was an impression made into melted red wax. As corporations were considered to have legal personality, they also used a seal – a company seal – in a similar manner when making contracts, signifying the directors' authority to enter the transaction. In modern times, seals are still used in some jurisdictions, although they no longer use melted wax. Where used, they are still a mode of authorisation which represents the authority of the company. If nothing else, this should be a reminder that each institution has its own modes of authorisation. In modern law, we tend not to spend much time considering jurisdiction as a mode of authority, let alone how law is authorised and represented. In part it is because we tend to consider legal form in terms of systems and processes rather than in terms of the visible representations of institutional activity. We tend to treat the representations of the authority, say the performance of an oath, the ritual of a court hearing, or the use of a company seal as incidental to modern forms of law. This brings us to the historical and critical engagement of law. In order to see clearly the ways in which jurisdiction is a practice of representation – that jurisdiction creates or establishes forms of legal relation – we need to view sovereignty as a particular practice of authority and not solely as a conceptual scheme.

Sovereignty and institutional form

Sovereignty is one of the most important ideas of modernity. It is a particular configuration of law and politics that emerged in Europe out of the religious wars of the 16th and 17th centuries, and the struggles towards separate temporal and religious rule. As we think of it, sovereignty did not reach its current form until at least the 19th century. Understood as the final and absolute authority embodied in a territorial state, it has intimate connections to other concepts: the state, the nation and territory (and territorial jurisdiction). However, if state sovereignty is the pre-eminent language of authority in modernity, it was not always so. Authority was exercised through a range of institutions, such as Roman Christendom, or the Holy Roman Empire, not just the secular state, although we usually do not think of these as exercising sovereignty in the modern sense.

It was not until at least the 16th century that either the terms 'sovereignty' or 'state' came to have the meanings that we ascribe to them today. Prior to this, their usage reflected medieval political, social and legal formations. A ruler could be sovereign, as could a husband or the Church. Sovereignty connoted authority (often political) but without a nexus to the modern concept of the state. 'State' itself referred to smaller political entities such as a German 'Stadt' or Italian city-states such as Genoa. Thus, in general, in medieval Europe, sovereignty was a personal political denomination, at its highest in the form of the monarch, and based on personal protection and obligation, but without the modern connection to a territorial state unit. Medieval Europe was a complex amalgam of hierarchies and territories through which authority was organised and exercised. These were not exclusive sovereign regions, but conflicting, overlapping, zones of authority, lead by diverse leaders according to shifting alliances and relationships. They took many forms: free towns, feudal networks and city states. Overarching all of these different political structures was Western Christendom and the Catholic Church. There was no strong distinction between secular and religious authority. Leaders exercised some brand of both, and religious institutions – churches, abbeys and monasteries – criss-crossed political lines and allegiances.

In the Middle Ages, significant shifts occurred in how many people thought about the relationship between religious and temporal authority. Over a period of several centuries, Europe was convulsed by wars seeking to define authority both between the papacy and various secular states, as well as between the states themselves. As the result of wars of religion, authority and sovereignty were recast. Much of this was brought to a head by the Reformation, and the emphasis of Lutheran theology on secular government. The Western Church as an overarching structure was in part transformed into national churches and the hierarchy of power in Europe, of which the Pope and the Holy Roman Emperor were the pinnacle, and was replaced with a new state based order (Beaulac 2004: 148–157). One of the tenets of new Lutheran political theory was that the Church was a purely spiritual body. Across Europe, this idea was used to legitimate moves by rulers and national assemblies to repudiate the separate authority of the Roman Catholic Church within their territories. Germany, Denmark and England all moved to lay sole claim to the right both to secular rule and to make ecclesiastical appointments. Ultimately, in a number of countries this resulted in the monarch proclaiming himself to be the head of the Church, rather than the Pope – Henry VIII being the best-known, but not only, example (Skinner 1978: 81–89; Act of Supremacy 1543). The result was both the transfer of ecclesiastical juris-dictional authority to the English crown, and the recasting of the Western Church, and canon law, into the Church of England and ecclesiasti-cal law.[1]

Much of the work of early modern jurists was to render law amenable to new forms of authority shaped through the jurisdiction of the territorial sovereign (Hobbes 1968; Bodin 1967; Pufendorf 1991). Older notions of authority as being superior power were slowly replaced by the conviction that sovereignty was the essential attribute of political authority (Hinsley 1986: 131–132) This new secular understanding of princely authority required new theories of the powers of the monarch and their relationship to law. We can phrase this in terms of the creation of new forms of jurisdiction and in terms of new forms of legal relationship.

For jurisprudence and political thought, the most important aspect of the modern state sovereignty became the ability to exercise full and exclusive jurisdiction over the territory of that state: authority and gover-nance were to be institutionalised within mutually exclusive territorial domains. This is often known as the 'Westphalian' state system because until recently it has been common to date the emergence of the modern sovereign state, and indeed the birth of international law, to the Treaty of Westphalia (1648), which ended both the Thirty Years War and the Eighty Years War. The Treaty of Westphalia (actually a series of treaties of peace) is said to have institutionalised the notion of the sovereign equality of states, and guaranteed to each state control of its own internal and exter-nal affairs. Whether or not the Treaty of Westphalia was a profound moment in the development of the current system is a matter of contro-versy. For many, it is orthodoxy that Westphalia inaugurated a new order. Others, however, seek to show that our state system had a more complex genealogy (Croxton 1999; Osiander 2001; Beaulac 2004). The term 'state' became synonymous with bounded territories and specifiable populations, and 'sovereignty' involved the assertion of independence: sole rights to jurisdiction over a particular people and territory (Montevideo Convention on the Rights and Duties of the State 1933, Art 1). What also needs to be noted here is that this formulation of authority is transacted by a transformation of the practice of jurisdiction. This is not simply a matter of recognising an absolute sovereign in the manner of a habit, covenant or contract. It requires the creation of jurisdictional and administrative arrangements in which such activities can be made meaningful.

Plural forms of jurisdiction and authority

If jurisdiction is concerned with the creation of legal relations, then we need to pay attention to the means and manner by which authority is bound to institutional life and through which someone or something becomes subject to the authority of law. As we have noted, one common way of thinking about this is through sovereignty – and in particular territorial sovereignty. However, this is not the only way to do so. This chapter looks to the plural forms of jurisdiction in the early modern period, which shows us several things. First, it illustrates the binding of jurisdiction (and hence authority) to institution. Second, it shows some ways in which we talk about authority and some forms of lawful life without taking a particular historical account of sovereignty as the main reference point or source of authority. Third, and in a slightly different register, the story of multiple jurisdiction, and its relative demise, provides us with an understanding of why sovereignty has become such a common way of thinking about jurisdiction.

Just as sovereignty in the medieval world looks foreign to modern eyes, so too does jurisdiction. As we outlined in Chapter 2, today we tend to think of jurisdiction as being largely a matter of procedure, either as domestic court procedure (in which court or tribunal should I initiate this action) or of conflict of laws (which country's law should be applied). However, jurisdiction had, and has, a more substantive role in law. While in modernity sovereignty is the lens through which we conceptualise or action authority in law, for much of the history of the last 1,000 years it was jurisdiction that fulfilled that role. Thus the primary jurisdictional question was which body of law applied to a matter – the common law or any one of its many rivals and companions: manorial law, stannary law and ecclesiastical law, to name a few.

For much of its history, the common law was one of a plurality of jurisdictions, each operating within its own largely autonomous realm, and with its own devices for attaching jurisdiction and hence for ordering its relations with other bodies of law. Each of these jurisdictions was an autonomous body of law, each with its own administrative arrangements, often courts, and its own procedures. There were, in fact, a bewildering array of such jurisdictions, most long forgotten. These were overlapping, frequently conflicting, operating at supra-national (to the extent we can think at this time of 'national' at all), national and regional level. They were secular and spiritual, common law and civil, or simply dispensing local law of a unique variety (Prest 1987). Some of these are well known and still operate in modern law, in particular ecclesiastical law, Chancery (equity) and Admiralty. Many of these courts did not apply common law, but administered distinctive sub-systems of local and special law. Altogether these bodies disposed of many more cases than the Westminster courts (Arthurs 1984). Many of these jurisdictions were quite small and specialised. Others, such as the county courts, were the most visible source of justice for many people.[2] In a time in which many people rarely moved far from their homes, it was these local courts which dealt with the matters of importance to people. These were, as Grey puts it, 'real courts with power to compel attendance and apply sanctions . . . They were forums for the practice of professional lawyers, operating with bodies of formulable, "learned" law. The matters they dealt with were important for the everyday lives of many people' (Gray 1994: viii).

The emergence of the new state-based political and legal entities in the late 16th and 17th centuries also led to a reframing of the relations of laws. In England, this resulted in a rethinking of the relations of the jurisdiction of the common law with these other jurisdictions. Most important in this shift was the break with the Catholic Church in Rome. No longer was the common law thought of (at least by common lawyers) as one part of a plural system, rather for common lawyers of Lord Coke's era it was taken for granted that the common law was the only system that England had ever had, and that the common law had to be defended against its rivals. It is from this time onwards that the common law becomes identified as the law of England (and of the territory), and eventually its national law. Other jurisdictions were now thought of as owing their authority to the common law (Hale 1971). Initially, the common law was literally 'the law of the land' as much of its early authority stemmed from its jurisdiction over land, and in particular freehold land. However, the idea of the common law as the law of the land began in this period to take on not only a public law aspect, but a symbolic aspect. The common law emerged as the law of the land and the law of the realm in the wake of the emergence of the English nation.

Territorial jurisdiction

To say that something or someone is sovereign or has jurisdiction is more than simply a claim of authority. Such a statement tells us nothing about internal arrangements for organising and exercising that authority (such as form of government or type of court) or even how that authority is exercised. Perhaps the most modern form of authorising legal relations is through the conjunction of sovereignty and territory. It ensures that in the modern nation state national law applies to all within that state. The mere presence of a foreign national in a particular territory, for example, is enough to confer an effective basis for proceeding against that person. Most states will assert jurisdiction over persons or events where any element of a matter takes place within its territory. Here we formulate and then reformulate the importance of territorial jurisdiction. We do so firstly to draw out the sense of the variety of forms of territorial jurisdiction and secondly to begin the re-description of the exercise of territorial juris-diction over its subjects – now population.

The work of the concept of territory can be understood from its etymology. Territory is derived from the Latin *terra*, 'land' or 'earth', and the suffix *torium*, meaning 'belonging to or surrounding'. Territory originally referred to the district surrounding a city over which it had jurisdiction. The term was initially applied to city-states in the classical world, and re-appeared to describe the jurisdictions of medieval Italian cities (Gottman 1973: 16). Thus, the term 'territory' was always connected to jurisdiction, but not to sovereignty. Sovereignty, in the form in which it existed in the classical world, had no explicit territorial link. 'Territory' also has an alternative etymology. The *Oxford English Dictionary* suggests that territory may also derive from 'terrere' – to frighten. This can be seen in the now obsolete 'terroir' (territory). Thus territory is also a place from which people are warned off, in other words an area of exclusivity and authority.

Territorial jurisdiction was not unknown in medieval England. In fact, lordships were frequently exercised on a territorial basis. However, 'territory' in this case did not have the 'public' aspect that territorial sovereignty has today. Rather, it was, as Keen reminds us, a kind of proprietary right (Keen 1991: 262). One example might be the franchise which was an area over which the king had granted jurisdiction to the territorial lord. In such areas the king's writ did not run. Each franchise had its own court structure. As forms of territorial jurisdiction, franchises differed significantly from the modern form of sovereign territorial jurisdiction that has dominated legal ordering for the last three centuries and illustrate one of the differences between early territorial jurisdiction and the territorial sovereignty of modern times. Territories can function on different scales. What characterises modernity is the predominance of the national scale over all others.

In contemporary idioms of national and international law a sovereign is said to exercise jurisdiction over a territory. Modern jurisprudence addresses jurisdiction through the topics of government and of population. In the idioms of political philosophy and jurisprudence we might then begin the investigation of legitimate forms of authority and consent to government, the institutional distribution of authority through forms of duty, offices of government and the aims of the state. These topics have formed the subject matter of both natural law and analytical jurisprudence for much of the last 300 years. It is still possible to compare Samuel Pufendorf's *On the Duty of Man and Citizen According to Natural Law*, first published in 1673 to John Salmond's *Jurisprudence* (the last edition he wrote was published in 1924; Salmond 1924). It is on this basis that we imagine the conduct of the affairs of state, the security of citizens, and the government of the welfare of population (Foucault 2003, 2007, 2008). Here we will not attempt to address this massive body of work of politics, government and legal ordering. Rather, we want to point to some of the broad forms of jurisdictional practice and then to indicate a variety of non-territorial jurisdictions through which authority might be exercised.

For present purposes we will note those aspects of territorial jurisdictional practice that we take up in later parts of this book. First, a jurisdiction over a territory is viewed in terms of the jurisdiction of courts and, increasingly, of states. Indeed, progressively through the 19th century we understand jurisdiction as the jurisdiction or authority of the state overall, with delegated authority being given to various judicial and administrative bodies (this is quite a change from *Prohibition del Roy* in Chapter 1, in which the courts are characterised as authority delegate of the king). Second, territorial jurisdiction gives spatial form to law. The territorial shape of jurisdiction is often linked to land, but it is important to keep the two distinct. A territory is a legal concept that may or may not have a direct relationship to land. For example, think of the complex formulations of borders and passports, and the determination of who can cross, dwell or work in a given place. These mark territory, not land as such. Third, in more complex ways, sovereign territorial jurisdictions provide the means of organising relations between laws. The traditional formulations of international law are both conceptually and institutionally organised around the forms of the sovereign territorial state. The conceptual ordering of international law around sovereign states forms the basis of membership of the United Nations. Despite many recent challenges to the paradigm of territorial sovereignty, it remains firmly at the centre of how we conceptualise legal and political authority. Global commerce, the rise of entities such as the European Union, claims to universal jurisdiction over torture or genocide, humanitarian intervention in Somalia and the breakup of territorial states, such as the former Yugoslavia, are all characterised as breaches in the bulwark of territorial sovereignty. However, claims of the end of sovereignty, and of the rule of geographically bound territorial jurisdiction, seem premature. There is not yet a viable global commercial regime, and while, for example, some limited extra-territorial scope has been found for institutions such as the European Court of Human Rights. The jurisdiction of this court is strictly limited and remains articulated around sovereignty.

In sum, we can argue that territory creates and maintains particular kinds of lawful relations. The most powerful are sovereign–subject (or citizen) relations distributed in territorial terms. We return to the significance of this observation in the final section of the chapter when we discuss substantive forms of authority, and again in Chapter 5 when we consider the forms and repertoires of legal persons. We can note here, for the moment, that critical approaches to jurisdiction tend to address forms of legitimate authority and expand such concerns into more general considerations of the form of law. For example, the work of Herbert Marcuse has given shape to our understanding of the links between authority and freedom – and turned our attention to the understanding of the deformations of the authoritarian character in modernity (Marcuse 2008); David Harvey has noted the ways in which our understanding of space and place instituted through law and the state have been 'flattened' and 'suspended' by networks of capital (Harvey 2001; see also Sassen 2008); and the research of Yvgeny Pashukanis, and colleagues, has developed accounts of the links between forms of contractual and property exchange and the commodity form of capital (Pashukanis 1978). All these approaches provide vital critical engagements with the abstract form of law. Here, however, we have drawn out something of the material form of the practice of jurisdiction. By concentrating on the conduct of law, our approach and concern lies with those forms of authority and freedom, that can be expressed through jurisdictional practices.

Ways of thinking jurisdictionally: four examples

This section looks then at four examples which show the different ways in which law is engaged when lawful relations are created and maintained through modes other than sovereign territorial jurisdiction. Each of the four examples – the *lex mercatoria*, ecclesiastical law, the law of the forest and the Court of Chivalry – have been chosen from a vast array of possible historical examples because they show different ways of organising legal relations, and could make us think a little differently about how we might approach some contemporary problems.

Lex mercatoria

The *lex mercatoria* is probably one of the best known of the medieval jurisdictions. The *lex mercatoria* refers to the law governing commercial interactions during the medieval period. In the past decade, particularly with the increase of e-commerce, modern commentators have increasingly looked to the *lex mercatoria* as providing a way of thinking about the regulation of commercial transactions which cross national boundaries and which often cannot be adequately dealt with by national law. Some commentators now claim that there is a new *lex mercatoria*: a new private system of governance for transnational business, one that is 'parasitic on' but not co-extensive with, state authority (for example, Stone Sweet 2006: 627–628; Ladeur 2004). There is, however, still disagreement about the scope and nature of this 'new *lex mercatoria*' and whether it really provides a model for rethinking modern transnational legal ordering (Teubner 1997).

The *lex mercatoria* has been described as 'not the law of a particular country, but of the law of all nations' (*Luke v Lyde* (1759) 2 Burr 882, 887; Zouch 1663: 89). Of course, it was not a law of all nations, not least because it arose at a time when Europe was still a patchwork of free towns and feudal networks. Rather, the law merchant consisted of a body of principles and regulations applied to commercial transactions and which was derived from the commercial standards and established practices of merchants and traders. It developed across Europe (and in some cases outside Europe) from the 11th century onwards, following the expansion of trade routes. These practices were often found to have commonalities with those of different areas, and gradually a uniform jurisdiction arose, based on reciprocity, and designed to protect traders from 'the vagaries of local law and custom' (Berman 1983: 342). The *lex mercatoria* was administered by its own court system. These were

attached to fairs and markets, and the law they administered was specialised and adjudicated by those who understood the rules of trade. Out of
the *lex mercatoria* grew certain institutions and practices which we
recognise today: standardised contracts based on good faith, promissory
notes and third party dispute settlement.

Although it has been represented as European-wide, the *lex
mercatoria* was subject to local qualifications, distinctions and exceptions
(Trakman 1983: 19). In England, the law merchant was administered by
the court of piepowder or *court pepoudrous*. Jurisdiction of these courts
was asserted on the basis of one's status as either a domestic trader or
a foreign merchant, rather than based on the more familiar mode of
territory. These courts had significant jurisdiction. The judges were the
merchants who attended the fairs, and the court's jurisdiction only
excluded pleas concerning land or pleas of the crown. There was no
monetary limit on the jurisdiction, and they could even hear cases which
had arisen outside of the limits of the fair. While the law merchant was
recognised as a law separate to the common law, the common law
adopted a number of its rules, and began to absorb that part of its work
which covered domestic transactions. In the 14th century, the jurisdiction
of the courts of the fairs was restricted by statute to matters taking place
within the limits and time of the fairs (for example, 17 Edw IV, c 2).
By the mid-15th century, much of its business had been taken by the
common law courts.

The emergence of the modern sovereign state, with its dominant
national legal system, helped to bind commerce to territory. Newly
emerging states offered traders enhanced security and enforceability of
agreements, but preferred their own law of contracts and their own courts
(Stone Sweet 2006: 630–631). By the late 19th century, international
commercial disputes were increasingly adjudicated by the techniques of
private international law ('conflicts of laws'), in which municipal judges
determine which set of domestic laws apply to a particular contractual
dispute.

The new *lex mercatoria* is making inroads into the 'post-Westphalian'
ways of ordering law. However, even its adherents acknowledge that it
is still parasitic on the state for enforcement. And even where scholars are
returning to the *lex mercatoria* as an example of how to think about transnational regimes, most still conceptualise the authority of this regime
within (or even against) the territorial sovereignty. It is this fundamentally territorial basis for law that the new *lex mercatoria*, like the old,
hopes to displace. An example like the *lex mercatoria* opens up questions
about what such a transnational commercial jurisdiction might look like

today and in the future, and how thinking about authority as jurisdiction might aid in formulating new transnational commercial regimes.

Ecclesiastical law

We have already noted the division in Western thought between the religious and the secular. A key jurisdiction in England in the Middle Ages was canon law. Prior to the Reformation, and for many years after, this body of law had a significant jurisdiction and a high volume of cases passed through the English ecclesiastical courts. At the same time that the common law of England was developing through the centralisation of royal justice, the Church was developing its own system of jurisprudence through the centralisation of ecclesiastical authority on Rome. The rules and pronouncements from Rome became a body of law known as canon law. In the pre-Reformation period, the canon law was received in England as the *ius commune* of the Church. Canon law recognised the Pope as the supreme legislator and judge of the Church, and was administered through a supra-national series of courts, including in England. English cases were frequently taken before the Pope (Maitland 1898: 122). Matthew Hale, Chief Justice of the Court of Common Pleas, for example, acknowledged the international character of canon law. Christian courts proceeded 'according to the rules of the ecclesiastical canons, constitutions, decrees, forms and precedents which were common to all ecclesiastical courts beyond the seas as well as here' (Hale 1971: 21).

One result of Henry VIII's break with Rome was the formation of the Church of England and the transformation of canon law into English ecclesiastical law. The canon law courts were incorporated into the framework of English national courts and into the framework of English law itself. The status of canon (now ecclesiatical) law remained unresolved after Henry VIII's declaration that he was now supreme head of the Church of England. This law was of profound importance to the way in which the common law viewed itself from the 16th century. It was against the canon law, and hence civil law generally, that Coke and others were defining the common law. The ecclesiastical law was suspect as 'foreign', while the common law was the native law of England.

Canon law remained in force as long as it was not repugnant to English law, and the Church was finally given authority to draw up its own codes of law by James I (Hill 1995: 6). In England today, the General Synod of the Church of England has the power to legislate by measure. A measure may relate to any matter concerning the Church of England and has the force and effect of an Act of Parliament once given Royal Assent (Church of England Assembly (Powers) Act 1919). English ecclesiastical law is now governed by a wide variety of courts and tribunals, of which the main courts are the Consistory Court and the Court of Ecclesiastical Cases Reserved. Many of the matters originally within the jurisdiction of the canon law are now under common law jurisdiction. The remaining ecclesiastical jurisdiction covers matters such as church buildings, offences by priests under the measures, and a criminal jurisdiction over holy orders in respect of doctrine, ritual or ceremonial, or conduct unbecoming the office or neglect of duty. Of course, all other criminal matters are now within the jurisdiction of the common law. Ecclesiastical law, therefore, remains a vital, albeit reduced, jurisdiction, with its own courts, remedies and sentences (censure being the most common). However, in the post-Reformation era it owes its existence to Parliament and the common law, rather than to the Western Church and the Pope, and is an integral component of the English legal system. It is the recognition of the state which maintains its quasi-independent existence. It is a part of national law. Marriage, divorce and wills therefore are now under the jurisdiction of state law – the common law – although the vestiges of their once separate institutional existence can be seen in the divisional structure of the English High Court, with its probate and marriage divisions and with its specific procedures. The re-alignment of the institution of canon law to common law has, however, had jurisdictional consequences. While much of secular jurisdiction has been assimilated to state law, some matters – those which require us to think about the traditional domain of church law – conscience – seem to have been left behind. Even the assimilation of marriage and divorce has been achieved by removing the 'moral' element (fault based divorce becomes no fault divorce; transmission of property can now occur regardless of legitimacy).

Human rights raise a similar and a new problem. Human rights seeks to re-moralise law, but the traditional jurisdictional place of conscience is no longer readily available. So, on the one hand, human rights are seen as moral rights which exist regardless of institutional jurisdictional arrangement (think, for example, of humanitarian intervention or even matters of *ius cogens* such as torture which transcend jurisdiction). On the other hand, state jurisdictions have attempted to shape human rights around patterns of due process, where questions of conscience are no longer substantive concerns. The formulation of conscience or jurisdictional spaces of conscience has become the most pressing concern of the institution of social life and the maintenance of a critical relation to civil and political authority.

Forest law

By exercise of the prerogative, the Norman kings of England declared tracts of land as 'forests'. Forest law shows another form of authority, this time a form of crown authority. What is interesting is the concerns around which jurisdiction is organised. Note the way in which Coke talks about this jurisdiction and its form. It is substantial. Importantly, the 'forest' was not a description of a physical place. Rather it is a jurisdictional place. A forest, according to Coke 'doth consist of eight things, videlicet of soil, covert, laws, courts, judges, officers, game, and certain bounds' (Coke 1644: ch 73). This was for the pleasure and recreation of the king (Manwood 1665). Forest law was intended to protect the 'vert and the venison' so as to facilitate the hunt.[3]

The forest law has been described in modern terms as a 'land use classification', but it was more. Rather, it was a jurisdiction under the control of a plethora of officers and courts, administered according to the forest law. It had its own institutions, separate to those of the common law, and its own specialised substantive law. Importantly, the jurisdiction of the forest was not primarily a territorial one. Rather, it was organised around a particular category of activity (hunting) and all required to support it. The king could create a forest by prerogative, but he did not become seised of all the land within. It could be owned by ordinary freeholders, who cultivated, hunted other species, or collected wood, although their use of the land was restricted by the laws of the forest. It was organised around the venison and vert. Other laws could and did criss-cross the physical territory where the forest was actually located. For example, with regard to matters of ownership, ordinary landholders within the forest would have invoked the common law or even other jurisdictions such as manorial law. Beasts other than 'venison' were not covered by forest law.

At first glance, the forest looked much like a modern national park: a place where activities are restricted (but not entirely prohibited) in order to protect the natural environment. Viewed through modern eyes there are functional similarities. However, its legal ordering was quite different. While the national park is dedicated and managed under state law (the common law, which uniformly applies to all within the park), the forest was an autonomous jurisdiction, a jurisdictional place in part beyond the common law, but one whose physical territory was never-theless criss-crossed by other specialist laws. It would be a stretch to conceptualise forest law as some kind of early environmental law. There was, after all, no concept of environment in the modern sense, or the worth of protecting the natural world. Nevertheless, something like the forest law gives us a way of thinking about how to give primacy to those matters – like the environment – dealt with badly by the common law. Within our system, environment is always subordinate to the logic of property (the traditional focus of the common law). Might forest law open a space through which we could rethink the primacy of environment around a different organisation of jurisdictional knowledge – an activity or an event?

Court of Chivalry

The final example is the Court of Chivalry, also known as the Court of Constable and Marshal. This was the court of the Constable of England and the Earl Marshal, who were the chief military officers of the crown, and who jointly administered the court. Although there is still much unknown about its origins and scope, it was a court of honour or chivalry and hence also known as the Court of Chivalry (Keen 1996: 135; Hussein 2003). In fact, the term 'chivalry' helps to better understand the scope of the jurisdiction, because it applied not only to matters of war, but also to broader matters of honour such as duels and armorial questions. It was in essence the court of, and for, knighthood. Like our other examples, what is interesting is the way in which jurisdiction is organised around a topic which looks foreign to modern eyes: that of honour (although for a modern example of honour as an organising category, see Appiah 2010).

Like the forest law, the substantial nature of this jurisdiction, and the topics encompassed by honour, can be gained from its definition. According to the *Monumenta Juridica: Black Book of the Admiralty*, its jurisdiction was over 'crymes, contracts, pleets, querelle, trespass, injuries and offenses don beyonde the see in tyme of warre between souldeour and souldeour, bytwene merchaunts, bytelers, leches, barours [etc]'. The book also makes it clear that the court had extra-territorial jurisdiction (Twiss 1872–1876: 281). While the court's jurisdiction was, however, often invoked in times of war, this was not a court of military law, nor was it the predecessor of the modern military courts or the source of martial law. This is a misconception arising from its later identification with early statutes of military conduct. When the court was revived under the Stuarts, it was this jurisdiction over honour, particularly in policing anti-duelling laws, as well as libel, which was exercised.

This extra-territorial jurisdiction was in sharp contradistinction to that of the common law which was bound to the realm. As the king's law, the common law was the law of the realm. In early modern law, other laws had jurisdiction outside the realm: most notably Admiralty and Chivalry.

As a result, courts across Europe, such as the English Court of Chivalry, claimed jurisdiction not only over their own countrymen, but they also had jurisdiction over aliens with respect to certain serious matters that took place in foreign lands where those matters involved the status and code of knighthood. The rules of honour were applied universally in war and could be considered a part of the *ius gentium*: a kind of universal jurisdiction. This jurisdictional ordering looks quite different to modern territorial sovereignty and the organisation of international law based on sovereign entities exercising exclusive jurisdiction over their own territories through a national law bound to that territory.

In modern law, we have no substantive category of 'honour', just as we have no substantive category of 'the forest': the scope of the Court of Chivalry's jurisdiction encompassed matters which in modern law make no sense as a category and which are dealt with quite separately. The court's jurisdiction covered topics which now are found in contract law, tort (libel) or crime (duelling is prohibited, but to the extent that to be engaged in it would trigger the criminal law). This is a matter we return to in Chapter 4. While not a substantive category of law, matters of honour and dignity are central to much of modern law: organisation of professional conduct; moral rights in intellectual property; and the regulation of death and dying in hospitals (we return to this in Chapter 5). It is not, therefore, that honour as a legal concept no longer matters, rather that it no longer has an obvious jurisdictional existence or practice. Indeed, the language of dignity has become a basis for many claims to universal jurisdiction, ranging from the defence of constitutional norms to the upholding of the universal mandate of the United Nations. Without a jurisdictional existence, dignity becomes a language of moral personality (Orford 2007).

These four examples have looked at a different way of organising legal knowledge. Each has introduced a jurisdiction centred around a concept or category which is different to the legal ordering of modern common law. The scope and address of jurisdiction for each differs considerably from that of modern sovereign territorial jurisdiction. By its very nature, sovereign territorial jurisdiction addresses everyone and everything within its scope. The *lex mercatoria*, ecclesiastical law, forest law and the law of chivalry and honour, by contrast, have substantial topics around which they are organised, each of which cross, but are not bound to, territory. For each, the institutional structures through which their jurisdiction is exercised are historically specific and the practice of jurisdiction is different. As seen, parts of these jurisdictions have been assimilated to the common law, while other parts have simply been excluded jurisdictionally. It is not that matters such as honour or conscience are no longer important to law. However, they are no longer attached to specific jurisdictional forms of engagement and hence lose their lawful character. This should not be taken as an invitation to jurists and jurisprudents to imagine lawful relations without jurisdiction. The work of Gunther Teubner has used the *lex mercatoria* to help re-imagine contemporary forms of the commons (Teubner 1997) and the work of Peter Goodrich re-imagines the 14th century courts of love as a feminine jurisdiction (Goodrich 1996). However, it is the courts of conscience that remain the most favoured jurisdictions of critics.

Representation

In the final part of this chapter we return to the material forms of authority and jurisdiction. Sovereignty, we have argued, is part of a jurisdictional practice – as can be authority. The authority of the crown or of the sovereign needs to be understood not simply, or only, as will or expression of an interest. It should also be considered in terms of the way in which authority is given its material (licit) form and in terms of the ways in which the king or sovereign is authorised – given both status and the duty and right, and power to act. Here, we want to emphasise authority as having visible and material form – it has a material practice which confers, represents and gives structure to authority. So, to take the example that we follow in this chapter, in the common law tradition it is the structure of the authority of the crown that is often said to encapsulate the varied forms of authority and jurisdiction through which we have inherited our legal thought. The corporate form of the crown is commonly described in terms of the doctrine of the 'king's two bodies'. The crown is split between the physical body of the king and the corporate form of the crown. While the physical form of the king will die, the dignity or corporate form of the crown never dies. The doctrine of the king's two bodies explains, or has been used to explain, a number of features of the continuity of the crown and of the status and office of the king. In 17th century England it was common to make a distinction between the king's immaterial and immortal political body and his material moral body. So, for example, the king as body politic and head of the political body of the realm could, as the king in Parliament, stand together with the Lords and Commons against the natural person of the king. In this way in 1641 it was possible for the natural person of King Charles to be tried for treason against the crown. The execution was against the king's natural body and did not affect the king as body politic (Kantorowicz 1957: 21–23). Or a modern example might be found in corporate law where we make a distinction between corporate legal personality and the individual and natural personality of the shareholder or company director. For us, though, it is also important to note the varied sources of authority and modes of authorisation that represent the authority of the crown. The king's two bodies turn out to be modelled on, or to echo, both a religious form – the two bodies of Christ – and a secular (temporal) form – the corporate form of office. We might, therefore, understand the crown as an assemblage of jurisdictions, offices and dignities. In the case of early modern kingship, therefore, the forms of royal authority were closely bound up with its modes of representation. Such modes provide both an emblematic representation and a technical means of authorisation. In modern times this is not very different. We can still understand modes of authorisation through their representations.

The work of the Zulu and African philosopher Mogobe Ramose has provided a powerful critique and reformulation of the concerns of sovereignty and kingship (Ramose 2007). In writing about the political settlement of the new South Africa, Ramose points out the ways in which it continues the old, bounded 'laws of conquest' and how these refuse parity to indigenous Bantu law and kingship (see Chapter 6). Ramose's political point is that claims to 'reconciliation' have to involve a restoration of sovereignty and title to land taken during the unjust wars of colonialism. A 'post-conquest' South Africa should be founded on the decolonised laws of African peoples. This is not possible at present given the denial of the authority of the pre-colonial Bantu laws of African peoples, and of the authority of kingship. Sovereignty here might still be territorial, but the territory which is understood through a relationship of kingship is not that of the territorial state. Ramose, for example, aligns kingship with *ubuntu* – the formulation of the oneness and interconnectedness of human relations. A relation between jurisdiction and authority need not run through European forms of sovereign territorial jurisdiction. For Ramose, the first condition of decolonisation is that it does not. As Kombumerri/Munaljarlai jurisprudent Christine Black has pointed out, in many indigenous laws and jurisprudences, authority and authority of law does not depend on Western sovereignty and the rule of law but the feeling for Land (Land, *Djang*; Black 2011: 9, 167–168).

Conclusion

This chapter has been concerned with jurisdictional forms of authority and the ways in which authority has been represented through law.

Jurisdiction has been presented as creating diverse relations of law. In developing a jurisdictional understanding of authority, and particularly sovereign authority, attention has been paid to the plurality of jurisdictional forms. To engage with forms of authority as questions of jurisdiction is to engage with the authority of law as an activity – the authority of the speech of law and the ways in which legal relations are created and expressed. Jurisdiction has been presented in this chapter as an instrument of law, but it has been argued that there have been, and are, a variety of jurisdictional instruments available to those working within the Anglo-common law traditions. In part, the narrative of this chapter has been presented to show the continuity and transformation of broad jurisdictional forms of authority and law. Thinking about jurisdictional form in terms of a practical activity allows for the diminution of sovereign centred accounts of law. We have not conducted a direct critique of forms of sovereign territorial state but have, instead, provided a number of resources with which to rephrase and localise its practice. By providing accounts of the plurality of jurisdictions, we have offered some sense of the historical specificity of sovereign territorial jurisdiction. By noting the material forms of authority, we have linked authority to the material practice of jurisdiction and, less directly, invited a reconsideration of the practices of legal authority and of the lawful relations created by and with territorial sovereignty. Paying attention to the jurisdictional form of authority does not provide ways of overcoming the state, but of putting the state in its place.

Notes

1   This is of course a complex story beyond the confines of this book. See, generally, Skinner 1978 and Brett 2006.
2   These are not the forerunners of the modern county courts.
3   Venison referred to a number of different animals, while the vert was the green plants which fed them.

References

Appiah, K.A. (2010) *The Honour Code: How Moral Revolutions Happen*, New York, NY: W.W Norton & Co.
Arendt, H. (1961) *Between Past and Future: Six Exercises in Political Thought*, London: Faber.
Arthurs, H. (1984) 'Special Courts, Special Law: Legal Pluralism in Nineteenth Century England', in Rubin, G. and Sugarman, D. *Law, Economy and Society: 1750–1914: Essays in the History of English Law*, Oxford: Professional Books Ltd.

Beaulac, S. (2004) *The Power of Language in the Making of International Law: The Word Sovereignty in Bodin and Vattel and the Myth of Westphalia*, Leiden: Martinus Nijhoff.

Berman, H. (1983) *Law and Revolution: The Formation of Western Legal Tradition*, Cambridge, MA: Harvard University Press.

Black, C.F. (2011) *The Land is the Source of the Law*, London: Routledge.

Bodin, J. (1967) *Six Books of the Commonwealth*, Oxford: Blackwell.

Brett, A. (2006) 'Scholastic Political Thought and Modern Concept of the State', in Brett, A. and Tully, J. (eds), *Rethinking the Foundations of Modern Political Thought*, Cambridge: Cambridge University Press.

Coke, E. (1644) *The Fourth Part of the Institutes of the Laws of England: Concerning the Jurisdiction of Courts*, London: E. & R. Brooke.

Comaroff, J. and Comaroff, J. (2010) *Theory from the South: Or How Euro-America is Evolving Towards Africa*, Boulder, CO: Paradigm Publishers.

Croxton, D. (1999) 'The Peace of Westphalia of 1648 and the Origins of Sovereignty', *International History Review* 21: 569–582.

Engel Merry, S. (1988) 'Legal Pluralism', *Law and Society Review* 22: 869–896.

Foucault, M. (2003) *Society Must be Defended*, Basingstoke: Palgrave Macmillan.

Foucault, M. (2007) *Security, Territory and Population*, Basingstoke: Palgrave Macmillan.

Foucault, M. (2008) *Birth of Biopolitics*, Basingstoke: Palgrave Macmillan.

Gaita, R. (1999) *A Common Humanity*, Melbourne: Text Publishing.

Goodrich, P. (1996) *Law in the Courts of Love*, New York, NY: Routledge.

Gottman, J. (1973) *The Significance of Territory*, Charlottesville, VA: University of Virginia Press.

Gray, C. (1994) *The Writ of Prohibition: Jurisdiction in Early Modern English Law*, Vol I, New York, NY: Oceana Publications.

Hale, M. (1971) *The History of the Common Law of England, and An Analysis of the Civil Part of the Law* (Gray, C., ed), Chicago, IL: The University of Chicago Press.

Harvey, D. (2001) *Spaces of Capital: Towards a Critical Geography*, Edinburgh: Edinburgh University Press.

Hill, M. (1995) *Ecclesastical Law*, London: Butterworths.

Hinsley, F. (1986) *Sovereignty*, 2nd edn, Cambridge: Cambridge University Press.

Hobbes, R. (1968) *Leviathan*, Harmondsworth: Penguin.

Hussein, N. (2003) *The Jurisprudence of Emergency: Colonialism and the Rule of Law*, Ann Arbor, MI: University of Michigan Press.

Kantorowicz, E. (1957) *The King's Two Bodies: A Study in Mediaeval Political Theology*, Chichester: Princeton University Press.

Keen, M. (1991) *The History of Medieval Europe*, London: Penguin.

Keen, M. (1996) *Nobles, Knights and Men-at-Arms in the Middle Ages*, London: Hambledon Press.

Ladeur, K-H. (2004) 'Globalization and Public Governance – A Contradiction?', in Ladeur, K-H. (ed), *Public Governance in the Age of Globalization*, Aldershot: Ashgate.

Maitland, F. (1898) *Roman Canon Law in the Church of England*, London: Methuen.

Manwood, J. (1665) *A Treatise and Discourse of the Lawes of the Forrest*, 3rd edn corrected, London.

Marcuse, H. (2008) *A Study on Authority* (de Bres, J. trans), London: Verso.

Orford, A. (2007) 'Ritual, Mediation and the International Laws of the South', *Griffith Law Review* 16: 353–374.

Osiander, A. (2001) 'Sovereignty, International Relations, and the Westphalian Myth', *International Organization* 55: 251–287.

Pashukanis, E. (1978) *The General Theory of Law and Marxism* (Einhorn, B. trans), London: Ink Links.

Prest, W. (1987) 'Lawyers', in Prest, W. (ed), *The Professions in Early Modern England*, London: Croom Helm.

Pufendorf, S. (1991) *On the Duty of Man and Citizen According to Natural Law*, Cambridge: Cambridge University Press.

Ramose, M.B. (2007) 'In Memoriam: Sovereignty and the "New" South Africa', *Griffith Law Review* 16: 310–329.

Salmond, J. (1924) *Jurisprudence: or the Theory of Law*, 7th edn, London: Sweet & Maxwell.

Sassen, S. (2008) *Territory. Authority. Rights*, Princeton, NJ: Princeton University Press.

Skinner, W. (1978) *The Foundations of Modern Political Thought Volume Two: The Reformation*, Cambridge: Cambridge University Press.

Stone Sweet, A. (2006) 'The New *Lex Mercatoria* and Transnational Governance', *Journal of European Public Policy* 13: 627–646.

Teubner, G. (1997) 'Global Bukowina: Legal Pluralism in the World-Society', in Teubner, G. (ed), *Global Law without a State*, Aldershot: Dartmouth.

Trakman, L. (1983) *The Law Merchant: The Evolution of Commercial Law*, Littleton, CO: Rothman & Co.

Twiss, T. (ed) (1872–1876) *Monumenta Juridica: Black Book of the Admiralty*, London.

Zouch, R. (1663) *The Jurisdiction of the Admiralty of England Asserted*, London.

Chapter 4

Technologies
of jurisdiction

This chapter is concerned with technologies and activities of jurisdiction. It is concerned with how the technologies of jurisdiction are engaged in the creation and arrangement of lawful relations, and with how the technologies of jurisdiction give us the form of law. In taking a critical approach to this central topic of law, we draw out the ways in which the technologies of jurisdiction represent the body of law and engage lawful relations. In many respects this is the pivotal chapter of the book. Without an account of the technologies of jurisdiction, there is no way of tying the institutional practices of law to the conduct of lawful relations – whether critical or doctrinal.

In this chapter, we switch attention from the authority of law to the practices of law. Here, and in Chapter 5, we turn to the practices and jurisprudence of jurisdiction. While Chapters 2 and 3 were about origins and forms of authority, this chapter is more concerned with how jurisdiction works – the practice or activity of jurisdiction. Jurisdictional thinking is quite rightly viewed as a technical activity: the question to be asked, however, is what kind of activity? Jurisdiction – as the power to speak the law – is not only about court procedure or about resolving issues of conflicts of laws. Nor is it concerned with what it means to reason in general. Rather, it is a specific mode of engagement of law. It is about how to do things with jurisdiction.

The technologies of jurisdiction we consider in this chapter are writing, mapping, precedent and the categorisation of law. All four are jurisdictional activities or practices and all provide important means of ordering law. Questions of the speech and writing of law engage the ordering of the time of law – its inauguration and transmission; those of mapping touch on the spatialisation and visual representation of law; while precedent and the categories of law concern the place of law, the former looking to the memory of law, the latter to the topics for disputes and the reasons for action. In this chapter, we are concerned with how these basic forms of legal knowledge and learning – the law discipline – can be understood as part of a jurisprudence of jurisdictional practice.

Our concern with drawing out links between prudence (or jurisprudence) and the technologies of jurisdiction lies with understanding the quality of lawful relations. What counts as lawful relations is not shaped solely by an absence of illegality, but through a positive engagement with the offices, roles, and obligations and rights shaped by jurisdiction. Lawful relations in this respect are shaped by the technologies of jurisdiction. In this chapter and the rest of the book, we take up this concern in a number of different registers. The first is by drawing out a relation between jurisprudence and the forms of jurisdiction and the second is by the consideration of the responsibility of form. In order to make sense of this we need to re-describe some of the ways we think about legal technologies and the forms of law. To do this it is necessary to draw out the sense in which the technologies of law are not simply technical but can be viewed as a craft or a prudence.

What then is craft or a prudence? Craft is allied to the concept of a technology (Foucault 1994; Sennett 1977). We use the term 'technology' because it connotes not only technique, but also encompasses the idea of devices and organisational strategies. Thus it captures the practice of common law jurisdiction. Technology derives from the Greek *technê*, meaning craft, art or strategy. In a classical sense, *technê* described a power or capacity to produce things whose eventual existence was contingent upon the exercise of that power; things whose existence was 'caused' by the craftsman. *Technê* (craft), as opposed to *epistêmê* (knowledge), connotes practical knowledge or practices ordered towards the production of something. There is, however, no strict dividing line between the two. Thus, craft is prudential because it works with, and produces, the kind of knowledge which is not scientific, but which requires judgment. For Aristotle, for example, *technê*, or craft, is also *epistêmê*, or knowledge, because it is a practice grounded in an 'account'. It is something which involves understanding (Aristotle 2002). While craft may seem an unusual term, it is in fact one that has been used by the American realists, such as Karl Llewellyn. They use this term precisely because they are interested in the combination of experience and technique which allows adjudication (Llewellyn 1960). While our central concern is not with adjudication or judgment as such, our concern with the repertoires of jurisdiction is closely related. As with adjudication, it is the combination of experience and technique that enables the practice of jurisdiction. Thus, for example, we discuss several technologies – including writing and mapping – which may be described as technologies of jurisdiction because they are devices or organisational strategies ordered towards the production or embodiment of a jurisdiction. In many respects, adjudication is a technology of jurisdiction. Here, however, we are not concerned with the work of judgment but with the creation of forms of law and lawful engagement.

Talk of a craft or prudence of technology requires some further explanation. The language of craft and crafting has always had an uneasy relation to law. It clearly relates to the practice or activity of the making and shaping of objects of various kinds. When we talk of craft in law, the language of craft might be viewed in terms of the creation and figuration of (giving form or shape to) lawful relations. In the way we are approaching law in this book, in the institutional version of lawful relations the figuration work of technologies points to the ways in which persons, places and events are bound to the body of law. The language of figuration also points to the representation of lawful relations.

Talk of craft emphasises that jurisdictional practices are active – the technologies of jurisdiction make or figure some relation. It might seem a little unusual to think of jurisdiction this way, but there are a number of accounts of jurisdiction which would not be too far from the way we want to think about jurisdiction here. One famous account of law as a craft and technology is offered by the jurist Lon Fuller. For Fuller, what counts as the craft of law was mainly directed to the sorts of practical–moral skills required in order to fulfil one's tasks as a lawyer well – primarily as a legislator. Lon Fuller's book *The Morality of Law* was the culmination of a long consideration of what Fuller called the 'inner morality of law' or an 'inner natural law' – the means and manner of achieving not simply order but 'good order' (Fuller 1969). For Fuller, there are eight qualities of making good law and for subjecting people to the governance of rule: (1) formulated as rule; (2) published; (3) prospective; (4) intelligible; (5) non-contradictory; (6) capable of being followed; (7) stable over time; and (8) enforced by officials. Critics of Fuller's arguments have tended to concentrate on whether such qualities are intrinsically moral (Hart 1958) or necessary for good law (Dworkin 1995) or for establishing the moral virtue of legality (or the practice of freedom under the law) (Simmonds 2008). Here we are rather more interested in the way in which Lon Fuller considers good order a matter of craft (his preferred craftsman is the carpenter; Fuller 1969: 96). Fuller opens up some important questions of the relation between the form and practice of law. First, and most obvious, Fuller's account of the eight desiderata or principles directs our attention to the purposes of legal activity. Second, Fuller's account is engaged with measuring the institutional practices of law according to a morality of aspiration – the procedures of law are directed to the development of the conditions of liberty and order (or with Ronald Dworkin – equality) (Simmonds 2008). Fuller's attention to the processes and procedures of law makes the consideration of the form and purpose of law central to the practice of law.

For many, Fuller's insistence that we think with the ideal forms of law does not attend to the practical concerns of contemporary legal ordering. For example, like Dworkin, Fuller expects lawyers to attempt to realise the inner morality of law in their work as legislators, adjudicators, and advisers. At times we talk too much about ideal forms rather than the plural forms and practices of legal processes, or that we judge only in terms of ideal or rational legal actors. Fuller's work, for all its concern with practical questions of law, assumes that law is a process that can be made to function well. This can blind us to the sense in which legal institutions often fail to attend carefully to either ideals of reason or to the practices of enforcement. In this book, we spend rather more time trying to hold onto material forms of technology in order to find out how they work. One of the weaknesses of Fuller's account is that it can appear to turn law into an ideal system which simply declares how things should be – particularly in matters of legal obligation. Fuller interests us here more for his concern with the practical work of figuring lawful relations through the use, and abuse, of the devices of law. A technology of law makes, or makes available, a certain way of doing or achieving things: a technique for conducting social and institutional life. So that law, rather than living up to, or failing to conform to, an ideal is better viewed as a technique that creates and makes certain activities or conducts possible (for more detailed accounts, see also Pottage 2004; Mussawir 2011). The ideals of law do not simply stand outside or above the conduct of law.

In this chapter, we address four technologies of jurisdiction: writing, mapping, precedent and categories. These, of course, are not the only technologies involved in the creation and figuration of law, but we have chosen them because they are central devices of legal ordering. Further, each of the technologies illustrates one aspect of the way in which jurisdictional practices actively craft law. For clarity, we have limited our discussion of each technology to one chosen aspect. However, each can do more.

First, we consider writing as a technology of jurisdiction. Writing is a material technology. It is a means of crafting a jurisdiction and lawful relations. Here, we focus on the ways in which the technology of writing creates lawful relations. For example, the common law writ commanded justice to be done, or someone or something to appear before a court. Engagement with law need not occur because of a formal court process, but can be because of something much more mundane, such as the issuing of a parking ticket. Writing not only inaugurates but also maintains law. It provides a means (not necessarily the only means) by which law is transmitted and communicated – across space and time. There are numerous examples of legal writing as a form of transmission – judgments, legislation, treatises and texts, and even forms. All of these inaugurate and maintain law. The second technology is that of mapping. Like writing, it is a material technology. Like writing it creates jurisdictions. However, here, rather than considering it as a technology which creates, we will focus on it as a technology of representation – a technology that configures lawful relations. Mapping allows the space of law to be represented and administered. It has a particular connection to one specific mode of jurisdiction – territorial jurisdiction. Mapping delimits the space and reach of law and it records the activity of the movement of law. It does so as a matter of the representation of a jurisdiction (but you need never have been there and may never go there).

The third technology is precedent and the doctrine of precedent. At common law, precedent is concerned with establishing and maintaining the authoritative sources of law and legal argument. This is so across Western genres of law, although here again we are predominantly interested in the common law. Here, we focus on precedent as a technology of attachment or binding. A technology of precedent might be thought of as binding a judgment or a case to the body of law. It is also one which provides a means of engaging or attaching someone, something, some event or activity to the body of law. So, for example, the doctrine of precedent tells us what falls within the definition of 'emotional shock' in the context of tort law. So those emotions, events or happenings which fall within that definition (as established by precedent) will be bound to law and the events which unfold will be amenable to legal judgment.

Finally, legal categorisation is a technology which names and orders legal knowledge. We identify legal relations by giving them names. This could involve defining certain forms of writing as contractual, it could involve trying to elaborate a general legal concept such as property, or it could involve considering what is included within a legal concept such as native title (a matter we return to in Chapter 6). It also encompasses the work of accurately trying to represent social relations in law. So part of the work of naming or defining homicide or genocide involves the

attempt to accurately represent the (moral) wrong of homicide or genocide. In a slightly different way, categorisation is also involved in the
organisation and ordering of legal knowledge. It gives us the means of
navigating our way through legal relations. How someone, something, an
activity or a place relating to law is a product of the way in which we
order legal knowledge.

What these examples of technologies of jurisdiction show us is that
jurisdictional thinking creates forms of lawful relations: the means by
which we inhabit law, and through which our conduct matters. So thinking about writing, mapping, precedent and categories as technologies of
jurisdiction shifts our attention to the practical activities which create and
organise the repertoires of our conduct and hence of lawful relations. (So
rights and responsibilities, for example, ought then to be thought of as
active relations.) Being practical means more than merely being technical. The technologies of jurisdiction gives us a kind of 'law craft',
showing us how not only to get on with making law work, but how to
think about making law work differently.

Writing

Legal writing has long been at the centre of disputes about the authority
of law and legal meaning. These disputes are extraordinarily wide-ranging
and reach back to the theological origins of legal thought (contesting the
nature of the divine word) and to the authoritative determination of the
scope of civil (state) authority (Berman 1983). This can be illustrated by
the disputes over the status of constitutions and constitution-making.
In some accounts of law the constitution acts not so much as a technical medium, but as a true source of authority. For example, for some –
'originalists' or 'formalists' – the literal wording of a constitution – in
particular, perhaps, the Constitution of the United States – carries the full
authority of law. For others, the words of the constitution gain meaning
and authority as shared political meaning or through legal tradition or
reason (Dworkin 1995; Fish 1989; Sunstein 1993). For those who interpret
largely unwritten constitutions (for example, New Zealand and the jurisdictions that currently make up the political entity of Great Britain), their
meaning is not carried in a single, or even multiple, document(s). Even to
the extent that written documents form part of the constitution (say cabinet
rules or possibly human rights instruments), these documents are treated
as evidence of meaning, rather than as having meaning in themselves.

When we are thinking about writing as a technology of jurisdiction,
it is necessary to remember that writing is concerned with more than

simply disputes as to meaning, or disputes about theories of interpretation (although of course these are important). To think of writing as a technology is to understand it as both creating and transmitting a range of lawful relations. In modern law, the most common way in which law is engaged is by way of a claim form, or statement of claim (which initiates a civil action) or a formal charge (criminal law). A statement of claim, or a charge, begins a legal action and engages the power of a court or official to pronounce judgment. It gives the authority to speak the law (*ius dictio*). But it need not be so formal. A simple example of writing as a device or technology is the parking or speeding ticket. If you park incorrectly, a parking ticket may be issued by an inspector and placed on a car windscreen. The issuing of that ticket engages law. It invokes the jurisdiction of the court and gives that court the authority to determine whether or not your behaviour was lawful or not. It initiates the jurisdiction, the speech of the law. Similarly, a speeding ticket, issued by a policeman, has the same effect. Stories are told of traffic wardens who apologise for having written a ticket, once an excuse is given, but drivers are told 'I can't tear up the ticket once it is written'. In our terms, jurisdiction has already been initiated and the law has been engaged. Someone has been 'called to law' (Althusser 1971).

But a statement of claim or charge (or parking ticket) is no ordinary writing. It is a written missive that transmits, that brings with it, the 'aura and authority' of the writer or issuer. It brings, inaugurates, transmits, institutional authority in its very form. It 'is no ordinary writing or warrant, no simple missive of everyday provenance but is rather a heavy sign replete with the full panoply of institutional obscurities, opaque lexical insignia, repetitions and the boredom of complex formal detail that attend to legal address' (Goodrich 2008: 214). As a technology and an activity, we can tie ideational disputes about the authority of law back to specific technical practices of legal writing. When we think of legal writing jurisdictionally, we expand our account of writing to the technical means of communication, so that a summons, for example, becomes a form of writing, rather than just the words on the form (Jackson 1988; Fuller 1969).

How does writing authorise as a technology of jurisdiction? As we have indicated above, these questions are subject to heated dispute. From the viewpoint of a technology of jurisdiction within the common law tradition, our understanding of writing needs to be expanded in another way. Tim Murphy has argued that the (common) law belongs within a 'scribal tradition'. For Murphy, the common law is 'not fixed in place by printed texts, [it] had, instead, its judges and their opinion of it' (Murphy

1994: 73). There is no text of the law, but rather a set of textual practices, whereby writing functions as a kind of evidence of law beyond the written. This can be contrasted both with an 'oral' tradition of law in which there is no task of inscription and a 'written' tradition such as civilian legal codes where law is expressed in the words of the written code.

Writing is not simply the interpretation of words, it gives us a particular form of legal writing that is connected to jurisdictional practice: arguments are made in court, supported by briefs; witnesses recount events in front of an open court. For most of the history of the common law, judgments were rendered orally only; no written judgment was produced. Both the transmission of law and the form of law depended on the memory of the judge. Judges could, and did, make decisions which relied for their authority on remembered cases, or remembered incidents, which were unknown to all except the judge.[1] Once reporting commenced, it was not the judge who wrote down the judgment, but a court reporter, who reported proceedings, often much later from memory, and then produced a volume of reports – hence the nominate reporters of the English Reports. Some of those reporters were judges themselves, remembering their judgments later. Transmission of law, however, does not occur just through law reports, but through more mundane legal documents – charters, contracts, land titles. Writing is not limited to some general way of transmitting law by evidencing it across time, rather, writing is a particular form that enables something to happen in and through law. It enables a certain lawful engagement with the life of law. An understanding that writing can be a mechanism for getting things going – for inaugurating jurisdiction – need not therefore rely on any idea that there are definitive texts. Legal writing in the common law tradition is linked to court room practices, not particular texts as in the civil law tradition (codes). Rather than relying on a definitive text, writing is a particular jurisdictional practice.

To draw out the significance of writing as a technology of jurisdiction, the simple example of the writ illustrates the way in which writing as a technology authorises a relationship with law. Throughout the history of the common law it has been the writ which brought with it the common law. The writ was a means of commencing or inaugurating an action: of bringing a cause, event or person to the law. Writs were a command from the king to appear in his court and to answer an allegation by one of his subjects. The need to purchase a writ reflected the 'superior' nature of the king's justice. Writs came in particular forms of words – and importantly only where disputes came within one of these particular forms of words could an action be commenced. The ability to get started at common law relied on the existence of an appropriate documentary form and of appropriate words. A certain number of writs existed, and each inaugurated a particular action. Where no writ – or appropriate form of words – existed, the common law had no jurisdiction. Writs did not encapsulate the gamut of everyday life. Only certain persons, places and events could be brought to law – and only if they could be fitted within a set form of words. A writ, therefore, did not create law in general, but rather it initiated a specific relationship of law. The limitations of only having certain writs was part of the impetus for the development of equity – a separate jurisdiction with its own jurisdictional devices. In modern terms, we have broad statements of claim – nevertheless, the common law still relies on the written form to get going.

The writ system was, of course, an institutionally specific device. Historically, many other jurisdictions inaugurated law not through the written word, but through speech. Some early courts commenced action through an oral plaint. The plaintiff would simply tell his or her story. The old county courts, for example, initiated actions until the 13th century, by oral plaint. But by the 13th century, they too had begun to imitate the written commencement of the common law courts. As the common law courts increasingly took their jurisdiction, they began to rely more on written procedure. From this we can see that because devices are jurisdictionally specific, they are themselves authorised by the very jurisdiction they inaugurate.

Much of the administration of modern law takes place through bureaucratic modes of writing – an obvious example is the form. Modern administration – the idea of thinking of law as a general system and of writing as simply being administrative – makes it harder to think of writing as a jurisdictional technology. The point we make, however, is that unless we hold onto writing as a jurisdictional practice we lose our sense of the authority and authorisation of law, and of how we inaugurate lawful relations. Writing is the preferred method of the common law (and of most modern law) of getting law going. If we lose this sense of writing as a technology of jurisdiction, then modern law becomes what Arendt calls government by no one (Arendt 1986), with the consequence that we no longer take responsibility for the form and force of our law.

Mapping

Mapping creates and makes lawful relations visible. Like writing it can be thought of as a material technology. As a technology of jurisdiction, mapping plays a part in the creation and representation of the visual form of authority. It helps with the crafting and representation of legal place by representing territory (and in other ways, persons and events). It is a technology that evidences the movement of a jurisdiction and a law – across land, between humans and between events. In doing this, it enables a relation between legal place and space, the ordering of people as populations capable of government and the assertion of jurisdiction over far-flung horizons. Obviously, as a device, mapping does not achieve all this by itself. It works with and through other technologies. However, in this section we want to take mapping as an exemplary jurisdictional practice of representation. It is easy to think of maps as representational in an evidential sense, but, as with writing, it is a little harder to think of mapping as jurisdictional in the sense that it crafts relations of persons, places and events.

It is not simply mapping, but the form of that mapping, which supports jurisdiction. Lines of latitude and longitude meant that unknown spaces could be given co-ordinates. The vast parts of the globe beyond the known world could be assigned locations by latitude and longitude. Despite never having been seen by Europeans, the new world could be mapped: the unknown became knowable and, more importantly, claimable. Territorial jurisdiction could be created out of the space of the unknown. Take a simple example. Governor Philip's instructions with respect to New South Wales confirmed the boundaries or limits of his jurisdiction – not only by subject matter – but by geographical scope. His jurisdiction was confined to 'our territory called New South Wales' (Joint Library Committee, Australia Parliament 1914: 1), which was defined as:

> extending from the northern cape or extremity of the coast called Cape York, in the latitude of 10° 37′ south, to the southern extremity of the said territory of New South Wales or South Cape, in the latitude of 43° 49′ south, and of all the country inland to the westward as far as the one hundred and thirty fifth degree of longitude, reckoning from the meridian of Greenwich, including all the islands adjacent in the Pacific Ocean, within the latitude of the aforesaid of 10° 37′ south and 43° 39′ south . . .
>
> (Joint Library Committee, Australia Parliament 1914: 1)

The limits of Philip's jurisdiction were reiterated in his Second and Third Commissions. Although Philip and the First Fleet had not yet departed for New South Wales, Britain was claiming jurisdiction over half a continent. At the time of Philip's Commission, the entire coastline of the territory of New South Wales was still unclear. In particular, the mapping of the coastline of the Gulf of Carpentaria was incomplete, as was the Great Australian Bight (Lines 1992: 16). Under international law, symbolic acts of possession, such as raising the flag, were insufficient to confer sovereignty. The position under international law was recognised by the British Government (Smith 1932–1935: 1). Despite this, the Commission appointing Captain Phillip as Governor conferred upon him jurisdiction over the eastern half of the continent, an area considerably larger than that claimed by Cook, including parts of the coastline and islands not yet seen by Europeans. Sovereignty followed in jurisdiction's wake.

This is a simple example of mapping creating and representing jurisdiction. In Chapters 2 and 3 we looked at representation in terms of political and legal authority. Here, we turn particular attention to the visual form and ordering of representation. Peter Goodrich reminds us that in many respects the Western legal tradition is a law of images (Goodrich 1995). It is concerned both with the licit representation of authority and with the representation of proper lawful relations. So, for example, we are used to royal and aristocratic emblems as being representations of authority. We are also used to the idea that they are restricted and regulated in their use by the law. Thus, they are not just images, but legal images. An obvious example is a diagram or map of the hierarchy of courts. Such a map would show not only the institutions themselves, and their jurisdictional relations to each other, but we generally understand that the courts with least authority are at the bottom, and the ultimate authority (the Supreme Court) is located at the top.

If we change focus and attend to the way jurisdiction addresses (or speaks) to its audience, mapping and maps are strongly, though far from exclusively, associated with the political and legal form of the sovereign territorial state. It is not difficult to think of a map of a nation state – say a map of the United States – as the representation of a political entity. What is mapped or represented is the territorial delimitation of political and legal authority. When we think of mapping as a technology of jurisdiction, we need to remember that jurisdiction attaches to the political and legal concept of territory rather than simply to physical land. As we noted in Chapter 3, territory as a jurisdictional mode may or may not map to a physical surface – in the way that the map of the London

Underground represents, but is not mapped to, the actual lines of the underground. In a rather more dramatic manner, the great jurisdictional division of the world by the Roman Church in the 15th century was accomplished by the delimitation of Spanish and Portuguese jurisdiction over the globe by reference to 'degrees' – latitude or longitude – despite the fact that they were unable to actually determine with any precision where those meridians were in relation to the physical land and ocean. This is still the case in the modern world. While GPS co-ordinates bring us more and more precise understandings of our place in physical space, they do not have any necessary relationship to the physical land. We return to this again, in the context of indigenous rights to land, in Chapter 6.

Attending to the links between mapping and territory allows us to appreciate both mapping as a technology of jurisdiction and the sense in which practices of mapping are embedded in legal thought. As a technology of jurisdiction, mapping gives us a visual representation of lawful relations. If we think of mapping as a particular activity, then we can see that our modern understanding of territory is strongly shaped by the process of mapping. For this reason, Ford called mapping the 'mid-wife of the nation state' (Ford 1999: 870). Any fight for national independence or any border dispute will attest the relation of peoples and places and is sharply understood today in terms of the representation of territorial forms. Maps in this sense are an important technology in the jurisdictional crafting of authority delimited by territory. When we think of mapping as a technology of representation, the categories of jurisdiction or jurisdictional arrangements provide a grid or scheme of representation that renders the world amenable to lawful relations. A territorial jurisdiction, for example, enables the configuration of lawful relations to be understood in a particular kind of way. Once engaged as a technology of territorial jurisdiction mapping does not simply represent land, it engages the ways people, places and events become subject to lawful relations. The technologies of the map and the plan provide the technical means of the conduct of government and of police.

However, the spatial relations of law are not, and need not be, viewed solely in terms of territory – or at least not in terms of sovereign territory (the territory of a nation state). It is possible to frame spatial relations in terms of jurisdiction of traders, scholars or police. While we concentrate here on thinking with territory, not all maps need have a primarily territorial schema. An example is the well known London Underground map. It is representational in character in two senses. First, as most know, the map is stylised and simplified. It does not relate to the actual train lines. It is a guide to getting around. Second, the map of the underground also represents a particular form of lawful relations. Those who travel on the underground enter into legal relations with the TfL (Transport for London) and they become subject to its authority. But this is not an exclusive jurisdiction. Travellers are also subject to the laws of the state, both civil and criminal. Whether it is a map of territory is open to dispute. It certainly is not a map of territory in the sense of being attached to the territory of the sovereign state.

The idea of the London Underground map as a jurisdictional technology is interesting for two reasons. First, we think of jurisdiction as only being about court officials and those engaged in court proceedings, as opposed to those engaged in everyday life and social phenomena. Second, we might be resistant to thinking of the London Underground map this way, because we tend nowadays to think of maps and territory as going together in a very literal way. In the pre-modern era, maps reflected the physicalised nature of communities' relationships with land and jurisdiction. The tradition of medieval mapping typically emphasised the sensuous rather than the rational and objective. In other words, 'the medieval artist believed that he could render what he saw before his eyes convincingly by representing what it felt like to walk about, experiencing structures, almost tactilely, from many different sides, rather than from a single vantage point' (Edgerton 1976: 9). The example of the pre-modern map makes it easier to see why the map of the London Underground is jurisdictional. What these maps lacked was what Ford calls the 'bright lines' of modern maps. It was the increasing ability to create maps that were precise which led to a particular way of relating to land, and hence to the creation of the different scales of territory (see Chapter 2). The precision of modern maps and their linking to territory give us a very particular way of thinking about mapping as a technology of jurisdiction and about how we understand authority within precise boundaries. It turns our attention away from the ways in which maps represent authority. While authority was often clearly visible in maps until the modern era, it is seemingly absent in their modern counterparts. It is clear that as an institutional practice contemporary jurisdictional representation of the territorial state makes extensive use of mapping. It is also clear that the uses of mapping are far from contingent matters of evidence or proof. They affect the substantive forms of the technologies of authority. They do so, however, without telling us much about either the sorts of relations that are created and addressed or about whether such relations are worth having.

Precedent

As a technology of jurisdiction, precedent is the skeleton around which much of common law thought is organised. Like the other technologies we discuss, precedent is broadly concerned with the proper means of the transmission of the authority of law. We are concerned here with presenting precedent as a technology that binds or attaches persons, places, events and activities to the body of law. Understood in this way, precedent is a hybrid technology: part technique of reason and interpretation and part institutional ordering and judgment. For the jurist, at least, it is these techniques that hold the body of law in place, and, for us here, enable the diverse parts of law to be bound in and held in place. The present orthodoxy tells us that we transmit and bind law according to authorised techniques of legal reason. As a technology of jurisdiction, however, we can take precedent as more than a technique of legal reason. First, precedent crafts and transmits relations of authority. Second, precedent binds relations to law. As a technology of jurisdiction, then, precedent gives us the means to assemble a body of lawful relations.

The common law has always looked to what has gone before. For much of the early period law was transmitted through the memory of judges, or seen as deriving from immemorial custom. Law was already there, it needed to be discovered in the past (this is still the basis of the modern declaratory theory of the common law) (Simpson 1973; Pocock 1957). In modern times, we still look to the past, but the authority of law is transmitted through the doctrine of precedent. The doctrine shapes law by stating (instructing) that a like preceding case should be treated as an analogy for, or justification of, subsequent cases. Generally, like cases should be decided in a like manner in order to ensure consistency in decision-making. Should precedent, therefore, be understood simply as rules for the authoritative and transparent transmission of law from one situation to another?

It is relatively easy to understand precedent as a technology of jurisdiction which transmits the authority of the law across time. A simple example is *Cadia Holdings*, a decision of the High Court of Australia (*Cadia Holdings v State of New South Wales* [2010] HCA 27). At issue was a simple question of the percentage of royalties to be paid on intermingled gold and copper which had been mined by Cadia Holdings. The answer to this question was dependent on the scope of ownership of minerals under the royal prerogative. In examining the crown's prerogative, the judgments started with the 1568 decision of the *Case of Mines*, reported in Plowden's Reports (1 Plowden 310 (75 ER 472)). That case set out those things which were considered by the law to be owned by royal prerogative: gold, silver, certain other minerals 'intermixed' with the gold and silver, money, whale, sturgeon and unicorn. According to the *Case of Mines*, one rationale for crown ownership was simply that as the king is the most excellent of beings he 'draws to it things of an excellent nature'. Another was the need to own metal so as to maintain a monopoly on the production of the coin of the realm, and to be able, therefore, to raise money for armies. These justifications for a legal principle seem quite foreign in modern terms, and are no longer perhaps even apt justifications for crown ownership. French CJ recognised this specifically. He noted these justifications and that despite the 'exhaustion of their relevance' that the principles on this aspect of the prerogative remain part of the settled common law (para 13). They are the transmitted authority of the law.

The doctrine of precedent is important on a number of different levels of institutional ordering. It provides a way of binding the reasoning offered in individual decisions into the institutional arrangements of the administration of justice. It does so by offering a detailed set of interpretative practices and administrative techniques through which to order legal relations. Critics of common law traditions contest two aspects of common law reasoning. First, they contest whether common law judgments are capable of producing a sufficiently clear account of a legal decision to determine or bind future use. In the 18th century, Jeremy Bentham criticised common law thinking for being 'dog law' – the common law is known only retrospectively at the point of being beaten (Bentham 1843: 235). For Bentham, this was reason enough to advocate for law to be figured in terms of legislation and not adjudication. In the last century, critics of law, especially the American realists, argued that legislation was also indeterminate in part because it required adjudication. Judgment, they argued, is indeterminate because it is not determined by a logic or rule, or rule application, but by a range of practical, social and political concerns. Second, and more profoundly, Kennedy and Unger have argued that the structures of modern law are conflicted and contradictory (Kennedy 1997; Unger 1987). As a consequence, such critics argue that all legal reason is infused with, and subordinated to, political or non-legal affects. Both sorts of criticism address ideas of law and try to judge them according to a principle and practice of reason. They consider the way in which the core practices of law provide, or rather fail to provide, justifications or explanations of how law proceeds. In the case of Kennedy and Unger the criticism runs even deeper: the structure of law and legal reason run against desirable versions of human life.

These are powerful criticisms. *Cadia Holding* did not discuss whether the authority on which it relied (the *Case of Mines*) was binding. But despite the age of the precedent and the 'exhaustion' of the relevance of its justification, the High Court felt not only compelled to commence its analysis with the *Case of Mines* but showed no interest in either reconsidering the justification for the original rule or dismissing it (although it did look at the effect of a later statute on the scope of the prerogative). For jurists such as Bentham, Kennedy and Unger, what is at issue is the quality of reason and the concern that contemporary reasoning is not capable of achieving the ends of law or justice. For these jurists, therefore, the reasoning in *Cadia Holdings* would be faulty. What should happen is better reasoning. What they propose is to transmit and bind law with a transformed account of legal reasoning: for Unger a 'higher reason'; for Kennedy a more honest reason. While we do not deny the importance of reason, for us such an approach deflects attention from the transmission of law, and that the transmission of law happens because we bind persons, things and events to law. The forms of argument about the binding quality of a decision are more clearly understood as a technology or craft rather than as a formal engagement (or misuse) of reason. The doctrine of precedent and the disputes over the reason of law can be understood as technologies that create, bind and attach lawful relations to the body of law. If we think of transmission as the transmission of reason, we are also tempted to think of the binding quality – or the quality of attachment to law – as also being connected to reason. However, we do not need to assume that all that is attached to law is attached by reason, or that reason is the only way to bind persons, places or events to law.

An example of how precedent binds persons, places and events to law, and how that law gets transmitted, can be seen in the question of whether there can be property in body parts. Modern debates over the commodification of the human body, patents on cell-lines and the human genome often begin for lawyers with a simple proposition: there cannot be property in a body or body parts.[2] Traditionally, this proposition is traced either to a decision of Edward Coke in 1613 in *Haynes Case* ((1614) 12 Co Rep 113; 77 ER 1389), although it is questionable whether Coke ever determined in *Haynes Case* that there could be no property in a dead body (in fact, he probably decided that a dead man could not own the winding sheet in which he was wrapped for burial); or to Coke's *The Third Part of the Institutes of the Laws of England* (*Third Institute*) (Coke 1644), 'the buriall of the cadaver (that is, *caro data vermibus*) is *nullius in bonis*, and belongs to Ecclesiastical cognizance, but as to the monument, action is given . . . at the Common Law, for the defacing thereof' (at 203). Like

Cadia Holdings, therefore, despite the fact that it is not clear that Coke ever said that there could be no property in a dead body, this is the transmitted rule – one reinforced by subsequent case law (*R v Lynn* (1787) 2 KB 733; *AB v Leeds Teaching Hospital* [2004] EWHC 644 (QB), [2005] 2 WLR 358) – and is a principle which still has considerable effect (Vines 2007).

The result of the acceptance of this rule, therefore, is that the dead body is not bound to law – at least the common law. It stands outside the jurisdiction of the common law – more accurately the common law declines to deal with the matter. It takes jurisdiction only in the sense that it declines to exercise it. But a careful reading of the above reveals that the *Third Institute* does not say that a cadaver does not belong to law, or even that it could not be bound to the common law. Rather, it says that in the matter of burial the body belongs to – or is bound to – another law. While the burial of the cadaver is *'nullius in bonis'* at common law, it properly belongs to the cognisance of ecclesiastical law. Therefore, while the common law might be concerned with the pragmatic matter of caring for the physical monument, it delimits its own jurisdiction to exclude what might be the sacred: the meaning of the burial itself. That is a matter for another body of law. The burial was a matter for ecclesiastical cognizance because most bodies at that time were buried in church graveyards, the domain of ecclesiastical law. Neither *Haynes Case* nor the *Third Institute* denies a body can be attached to law – specifically to the body of the common law. But in neither case was the body itself ever at issue. In the ecclesiastical jurisdiction the concern is with conscience and the transmission of the soul. The common law jurisdiction deals with external matters of government. Despite the very particular situation of this dispute, Yan Thomas, for example, has similarly pointed to the way that Roman law also made of use of technical accounts to keep apart (or in relation) the sacred and the profane in law (Thomas 2004).

In modern law, ownership of body parts has two jurisdictional aspects. First, the transmission of the rule – now one of precedent – that there is no property in a dead body. Second, and more problematically, as the common law declines jurisdiction there is no longer any meaningful ecclesiastical jurisdiction to provide a body of law to which the body could otherwise be bound.[3] The consequence of the failure to bind the body to the common law, the way in which precedent transmits law across time, and the effective demise of non-common law jurisdictions (see Chapter 2), has been to leave the dead body poorly bound to law.

The principle that a dead body – or body parts at all – cannot be the subject of ownership continues to cause difficulties for thinking about how one engages lawful relations in areas such as patenting cell-lines or other medical technologies derived from the human body. This is because there is no consideration of the jurisdictional character of *Haynes Case*. Instead, it has proven necessary to find other resources of argument to explain how a (dead) body becomes bound to law. Here we note that the problem of *Haynes Case* does not seem to be that of *Cadia Holdings*. If *Cadia Holdings* accepts a very thin account of what is held and carried by law or what is bound by precedent, then *Haynes Case* struggles with what can be inherited through a jurisdiction or what happens when we join what were two distinct jurisdictions.

In this section we have emphasised precedent as a technology of transmission. We have investigated a number of ways in which the doctrine of precedent, and judgment through precedent, has shaped the quality of transmission of law and what is bound into law. In doing this we have emphasised that precedent is not simply an account of the transmission of reason, but also requires a sense of the way in which transmission is also an engagement of institution and a concern with the address of law. In *Cadia Holdings* the failure to address the quality of transmission also resulted in a loss of legal form and a loss of ability to take responsibility for legal judgment. (If the visible authority and the dignity of the crown is really 'exhausted' can a court live without it? Or is it enough to continue to act with an empty form?) We also saw the way that the court in *Haynes Case* lost the mode and meaning of what is bound to law. Failure to attend to this aspect of precedent threatens to leave us with an account of precedent that is concerned with the administration of precedents rather than the ordering of forms of life.

Categories

Questions of categorisation rest at the centre of theology, law, arts and the sciences. Attending to categories is, in many ways, the central task of the office of the jurist. This work could involve defining certain forms of writing as contractual, certain acts as criminal, or it could involve trying to elaborate a general legal concept such as property. Traditionally, this has been cast in terms of legal science or legal knowledge. This is not the only way to understand the work of categorisation, however, as it is also a technology of jurisdiction. Categorisation creates and crafts the forms of lawful relations. With it we name, locate and order the body of law; we devise ways of engaging forms of law; and we address the order of justice. An example is the creation and naming of a distinction between a criminal or a civil matter. This distinction can be understood as a conceptual distinction between the nature of a criminal wrong (say a matter of relation between the state and its subjects or citizens) and a civil wrong (say a matter of relation between subjects or citizens).

In the final section of this chapter, we consider what is contained and carried through the practice of categorisation as a technology of jurisdiction. Within the common law, legal knowledge was predominantly organised around the forms of action and the writ system. In thinking about our present modes of categorisation, two important jurisdictional moments were the abolition of the forms of action and the writ system and the ending of some of the older (non-common law) jurisdictions and their courts. These two events together led to the reorganisation of legal knowledge in the late 19th and early 20th centuries, resulting in many of the domains of law familiar to us now. The particular histories of the forms of action and the re-ordering of the administrative jurisdictions of the courts have made categorisation a distinct technology of jurisdiction. As will be discussed, the reorganisations of the period contributed towards the current way in which we think about jurisdiction – as simply a procedural or technical, rather than substantive, concern. The question which we follow here is where in modern law is the substance of law named and located?

As noted above, two of the significant jurisdictional events of the 19th century were the abolition of the forms of action, and the demise of many of the surviving non-common law jurisdictions. The (possibly unexpected) result of these was both the reorganisation of legal knowledge and the (re-)location of the substance of law to the categories of law. At common law, forms of action were intimately connected to the writ. As we discussed in the first part of this chapter, at common law each action needed to be commenced by a writ. It was not enough that a wrong had been committed against you. The facts needed to fit into one of the set causes of actions and be started by the writ for that cause of action. If there was no appropriate writ and cause of action, then the common law had no jurisdiction. As Maitland said, choice of writ was a 'choice between methods of procedure adapted to cases of different kinds' (Maitland 1965: 2). Each of the writs, or forms of action, can be thought of as a pigeon-hole (Maitland 1965: 4). Over time, substantive law grew up around each of these writs, within the pigeon-hole of the particular form of action. In short, it was the form of action that held substantive legal relations in place. It did so by providing the material actions or practices that bring a person to law and that name the wrongs or injuries that can be brought to law. Conversely, such naming marks the limits of what can be recognised in law as an injury or wrong. Unless the injury or wrong could be brought within one of the causes of action then it remained without a remedy – outside law, not amenable to law. In this, the forms of action join the assemblage of technologies of writing, mapping and precedent that figure the institutional life of law.

The forms of action at common law were not the only means of naming legal relations in England. Each jurisdiction had its own way of initiating and naming legal relations. The changing institutional form of such jurisdictions has transformed not only the institutional form of law, but also the ways in which legal relations are created and understood. In the 19th century, there were a variety of alternative, non-common law, jurisdictions still in existence. In the first half of the 19th century, it was still possible and common, therefore, to speak of jurisdictions in the plural, although many non-common law jurisdictions had either been absorbed by the common law or become moribund (Thompson 1975). While not overstating the matter, it was still the case that the laws which governed disputes and regulated peoples' rights were not always those of the common law and the other courts of the land still adjudicated much law (Arthurs 1984: 384). As a result, the primary question of jurisdiction, and of whose authority, was still of importance. There was no automatic assumption that the body of rules and principles known as the common law would apply to any dispute – that the jurisdiction of the common law would be the site of authority and determination in all matters. In the mid- to late 19th century, however, many of the last of the non-common law jurisdictions were abolished to make way for the new, centralised, county court system (County Courts Amendment Act 1867, s 28). As a result, the common law courts became the automatic starting point for almost all actions. This legal centralisation was furthered by the Judicature Acts 1873 and 1875. Now, rather than asking 'Which writ?', 'Which court?' and 'Which jurisdiction?', a new set of questions arose that drew apart relations between questions of jurisdiction and those of categorisation and classification. Jurisdictional questions were increasingly expressed in terms of the administration and ordering of a single common law jurisdiction. The de-emphasis of the common law as a jurisdictional body led eventually to the loss of any conception of jurisdiction beyond the strictly procedural questions associated with courts and monetary limits. With the pre-eminence of the common law there was no challenge to its jurisdiction, and hence no longer any need to think about the jurisdiction of the common law or indeed of the particular configuration of lawful relations within the common law jurisdiction or between the common law and any other jurisdiction.

By the 19th century, not only had significant bodies of substantive common law developed, particularly in the areas of contract and crime, but in some of these areas, despite the forms of action, that law had already begun to take on its modern form. By 1800, for example, contract had emerged as an abstract entity, with a structure which was distinct from the forms of action. Tort, on the other hand, remained divided between trespass and case, and a large 'residuary group linked together by nothing stronger than that the defendant was alleged to have caused loss to the plaintiff' (Ibbetson 1999: 215). Negligence had begun to emerge, but much of this residual group consisted of a series of specific duties owned to specific classes of plaintiff, rather than a general principle of duty of care. Nor was tort fully separated from contract. Property remained bifurcated: the division between real and personal property was (and still is) central to property law. Thus, while much significant substantive law had developed, the abolition of the forms of action made space for the unification of different parts of law which still subsisted within the interstices of the particular forms of pleading. While the reorganisation of legal categories had already begun by the time of the abolition of the forms of action, their abolition provided a conceptual space in which academics and jurists could seriously begin to think about how to organise substantive law. A new technology was needed to bind an account of lawful relations to a body of law. Since the late 19th century, the ways of naming lawful relations have become more varied, as have the sites or places of dispute or contest of lawful relations. The substance of law has been re-located through the devising of new forms of legal categorisation.

One way to look at the emergence of the new categories of law is through the textbook tradition. The impact of university jurists on the reconfiguring of the law was important. Contract, criminal law and administrative law, for example, all largely received their current shape through the endeavours of university jurists. Textbooks (or their cousins, treatises) allow observation of the changes in the shape and organisation of the law, and reflect new classificatory endeavours as well as influential court determinations. Two simple examples might suffice here. In the first half of the 19th century, tort law (in the sense in which it then existed) was a range of actions – most commonly trespass, trespass on the case and trover. American jurists and academics, and in particular Oliver Wendell Holmes, did much in the wake of the abolition of the forms of action to reformulate tort into its current category.[4] In his 1873 essay 'A Theory of Torts' Holmes proposed a new structure for tort law, and placed accidental injury as the primary domain of torts – 'a focus which has continued to shape our view of the field ever since' (Grey 2001: 1232). In England, even before the abolition of the forms of action was complete, James FitzJames Stephen's *A General View of the Criminal Law of England* (1863) combined what had previously been the laws of public wrongs and the pleas of the Crown and, in so doing, turned the 'laws of crime to criminal law' (Rush and McVeigh 1997).[5]

If the substance of law is not that of the common law (or any other jurisdiction), where now, then, is the substance of law to be addressed? One answer is that jurisdiction and its substance can be thought of through the modern juristic formulation of legal categories. The jurisdictional question now, rather than 'Which jurisdiction?' (common law or something else), is 'Is it in the domain of tort?' or 'Is it in the domain of contract?'. It is through the use of terms like 'domain' that the jurisdictional work of categorisation is recognised. The reformulation of the jurisdictional practice of categorisation in terms of 'domains of law' has had a number of consequences. The first of these is that the juristic work of concept formation has itself become a technology or practice of jurisdiction – categories name, order and locate lawful relations; they determine the points of institutional limit; and they offer an account of the substance of law. The legal concept of tort is now required to do the work of jurisdictional categorisation. This frequently obscures the jurisdictional work of crafting lawful relations. A second consequence is that once the work of categorisation is undertaken through conceptual schemes of jurists, some questions of jurisdiction became diffuse and difficult to locate (Douzinas and Geary 2005; Murphy 1997). Much of the criticism of modern administrative and bureaucratic forms of government has been precisely directed at the sense that it is no longer meaningful to ask questions like 'Whose law?', 'Which authority?' and 'With what limits?'.

Finally, it is worth noting that in the common law tradition some formulations of 'domain' and 'concept' work better than others in engaging categorisation as a technology of jurisdiction. Take, for example, the modern understanding of human rights. Human rights as a juristic category is new. It has developed in international law only over the last 75 years. It is a commonplace of legal thought that human rights carry the ambiguity of both substance and address. Human rights have a moral and political valence that is not contained in legal form. To frame matters in this way, however, loses the jurisdictional character of what is at issue. As a legal category, human rights perform the task of conceptual ordering and act as a jurisdictional 'domain'. It is through the legal form of human rights that we name, order and locate lawful relations. Human rights are addressed to states or to humanity with the demand that rights be recognised or duties fulfilled. Such categorisation, however, does not readily address or answer questions of the jurisdictional domain of human rights. Nor does it respond to the question of authority and of 'Whose law?'.

Conclusion

We opened this chapter with a brief consideration of the work of Lon Fuller. Fuller's work is interesting for us for two reasons. The first, most clearly, is that his work directly ties the understanding of legal process to the activity of crafting lawful relations. (It is his answer to the problem of how to create lawful relations and good order that makes Fuller an important jurist, rather than his answer to the question 'What is law?'.) However, our account has differed from that of Fuller and other 'process' thinkers like Ronald Dworkin, in that we have linked our account of process to jurisdictional practices rather than to rational forms. In doing this, we have not offered an account of the legal system as a whole, but of specific identifiable practices. In so doing we have argued that it is the technologies of jurisdiction that figure or give form to law. In this chapter, we have tracked the work of four technologies: writing, mapping, precedent and categories. In presenting these as practices, we have linked them to some of the traditional concerns of common law jurisprudence: transmission, representation, binding and naming.

Viewing jurisdiction in terms of the crafting of lawful relations allows for a consideration of relations between authority and freedom. Our account, then, differs from that of Fuller in two ways. The first lies with the tradition of interpretation that links the craft of process to interpretation, and the second with the sense of the perfection of law and of the forms of life that can be lived through law. Fuller shapes his account of the practice of law and of authority (subjecting people to governance) around an ideal form of good ordering. In doing this, he joins a long established tradition of jurisprudence and interpretation inherited from medieval jurisprudence that is concerned with the relation between a principle of order (*ordo ordinans*) and what is being ordered (*ordo ordinatus*). In medieval theology and jurisprudence, these concerns are linked to the relation between divine and mundane order and the characterisation of the spiritual and temporal realms. Fuller places these arguments inside law. The task of the jurist craftsman is to realise (and perfect) forms of good legal order. In this chapter, we have linked the practices of technology to the transmission, representation, binding and naming of lawful relations. This owes more to a concern with the conduct of lawful relations than to ideal forms of authority. We have considered how the technologies of jurisdiction have created practices of association. To some extent, presenting jurisdiction and the shape of the common law tradition as a practice disenchants lawful relations. This has allowed us to raise a question about the 'responsibility of form'. Attending to the modern practice of jurisdiction in the common law opens for critical evaluation the ways in which our contemporary jurisdictional practices create lawful relations that are not meaningful or adequate to the tasks that need to be addressed as a matter of justice (legal or otherwise). We also noted the sense in which it is harder to see the way in which modern forms of legal writing, mapping, precedent and categorisation create lawful relations. Modern administrative forms of law pay relatively little attention to jurisdictional relations between the authority of law and the practice of government of action. In this we join our discussion of the technologies of jurisdiction with the modern concern with the deleterious effects of technology and the creation or loss of forms of authority (Arendt 1961).

Notes

1 For an example, see the decision of Lord Mansfield in *Mostyn v Fabrigas* (1774) 1 Cowp 161 on the jurisdiction of the English common law courts over local matters in the remote colonial outpost of Newfoundland.
2 See the skill and care exception: *Doodeward v Spence* (1908) 6 CLR 406; *R v Kelly* [1999] QB 621. And, for a recent extension, see *Yearworth v North Bristol NHS Trust* [2009] EWCA Civ 37 – ownership of excised or otherwise separated body parts could be property for the purposes of a negligence action (here ejaculated sperm).
3 In England, as we noted in Chapter 3, ecclesiastical (or Anglican church law) still has some limited jurisdiction, although it would not be thought any longer to be a jurisdiction independent of the common law. One aspect of its remaining authority is the question of right to burial – or removal of a body – in and from a church graveyard.
4 The abolition of the forms of action in this context can be more directly traced to the New York Field Code of 1848. By the time Holmes reformulated torts, some 20 US states had followed suit and replaced the forms of action with one civil action.
5 The Common Law Procedure Act 1852 commenced the process of removing the forms of action by providing that it was no longer necessary to state the form of action in the originating summons. The abolition was completed by the Judicature Acts.

References

Althusser, L. (1971) 'Ideology and Ideological State Apparatuses', in Althusser, L. and Brewster. B. (eds), *Lenin and Philosophy and Other Essays*, New York, NY: Monthly Press.

Arendt, H. (1961) *Between Past and Future: Six Exercises in Political Thought*, London: Faber.

Arendt, H. (1986) *The Origins of Totalitarianism*, London: Deutsch.

Aristotle (2002) *Nicomachean Ethics* (Rowe, C. trans; Brodie, S. ed), Oxford: Oxford University Press.

Arthurs, H. (1984) 'Special Courts, Special Law: Legal Pluralism in Nineteenth Century England', in Rubin, G. and Sugarman, D. (eds), *Law, Economy and Society: 1750–1914: Essays in the History of English Law*, Oxford: Professional Books Ltd.

Bentham, J. (1843) *The Works of Jeremy Bentham*, vol 5, Edinburgh: William Tait.

Berman, H. (1983) *The Formation of the Western Legal Tradition*, Cambridge, MA: Harvard University Press.

Coke, E. (1644) *The Third Part of the Institutes of the Laws of England: concerning high treason, and other pleas of the crown, and criminal causes*, London: M. Flesher, for W. Lee, and D. Pakeman.

Douzinas, C. and Geary, A. (2005) *Critical Jurisprudence*, Oxford: Hart Publishing.

Dworkin, R. (1995) *Life's Dominion: An Argument about Abortion and Euthanasia, and Individual Theory*, London: Harper Collins.

Edgerton, S. (1976) *The Renaissance Re-discovery of Linear Perspective*, New York, NY: Harper & Row.

Fish, S. (1989) *Doing What Comes Naturally: Change, Rhetoric, and the Practice of Theory in Literary and Legal Studies*, Durham, NC: Duke University Press.

Ford, R. (1999) 'Law's Territory (A History of Jurisdiction)', *Michigan Law Review* 97: 843–930.

Foucault, M. (1994) 'Space, Knowledge, Power', in Faubion, J. (ed), *Power: Essential Works of Foucault 1954–1984*, New York, NY: Penguin.

Fuller, L. (1969) *The Morality of Law*, New Haven, CT: Yale University Press.

Goodrich, P. (1995) *Oedipus Lex: Psychoanalysis, History, Law*, Berkley, CA: University of California Press.

Goodrich, P. (2008) 'Visive Powers: Colours, Trees and Genres of Jurisdiction', *Law and Humanities* 2: 213–231.

Grey, T. (2001) 'Accidental Torts', *Vanderbilt Law Review* 54: 1225–1284.

Hart, H.L.A. (1958) 'Positivism and the Separation of Law and Morals', *Harvard Law Review* 71: 593–629.

Ibbetson, D. (1999) *A Historical Introduction to the Law of Obligations*, Oxford: Oxford University Press.

Jackson, B. (1988) *Law, Fact and Narrative Coherence*, Roby: Charles Deborah Publications.

Joint Library Committee, Australia Parliament (1914) *Historical Records of Australia, Series I: Governor's Despatches To and From England*, Governor Phillip's First Commission, King George III to Arthur Phillip, 12 October 1786, Vol 1, Sydney: The Library Committee of the Commonwealth Parliament, Sydney.

Kennedy, D. (1997) *A Critique of Adjudication (fin de siecle)*, Cambridge, MA: Harvard University Press.

Lines, J. (1992) *Australia on Paper: The Story of Australian Mapping*, Box Hill: Fortune Publications.

Llewellyn, K. (1960) *The Common Law Tradition: Deciding Appeals*, Boston: Little Brown & Company.

Maitland, M. (1965) *The Forms of Action At Common Law*, Cambridge: Cambridge University Press, Cambridge.

Murphy, T. (1994) 'As If: Camera Juridica', in Douzinas, C., Goodrich, P. and Hachamovitch, Y. (eds), *Politics, Postmodernity and Critical Legal Studies: The Legality of the Contingent*, London: Routledge.

Murphy, T. (1997) *The Oldest Social Science: Configurations of Law and Modernity*, Oxford: Clarendon Press.

Mussawir, E. (2011) *Jurisdiction in Deleuze: The Expression and Representation of Law*, Abingdon: Routledge-Cavendish.

Pocock, J.G.A. (1957) *The Ancient Constitution and the Feudal Law: A Study of English Historical Thought in the Seventeenth Century*, Cambridge: Cambridge University Press.

Pottage, A. (2004) *Law, Anthropology and the Constitution of the Social*, Cambridge: Cambridge University Press.

Rush, P. and McVeigh, S. (1997) 'Cutting Our Losses: Criminal Legal Doctrine', in Rush, P., McVeigh, S. and Young, A. (eds) (1997), *Criminal Legal Doctrine*, Aldershot: Ashgate.

Sennett, R. (1977) *The Fall of Public Man*, New York, NY: Alfred A Knopf.

Simmonds, N. (2008) *Central Issues in Jurisprudence*, 3rd edn, London: Sweet & Maxwell.

Simpson, A.W.B. (1973) 'The Common Law and Legal Theory', in Simpson, A.W.B. (ed), *Oxford Essays in Jurisprudence*, 2nd Series, Oxford: Oxford University Press.

Smith, H. (ed) (1932–1935) *Great Britain and the Law of Nations: A Selection of documents illustrating the views of the government in the United Kingdom upon matters of International Law*, Vol II, London: King.

Sunstein, C. (1993) *The Partial Constitution*, Cambridge, MA: Harvard University Press.

Thomas, Y. (2004) '*Res Religiosi:* On the Categories of Religion and Commerce in Roman Law', in Pottage, A. and Mundy, M. (eds), *Law, Anthropology, and the Constitution of the Social: Making Persons and Things*, Cambridge: Cambridge University Press.

Thompson, E.P. (1975) *Whigs and Hunters: the Origin of the Black Act*, New York, NY: Pantheon Books.

Unger, R. (1987) *Plasticity into Power: Comparative Historical Studies on the Institutional Conditions of Economic and Military Success*, Cambridge: Cambridge University Press.

Vines, P. (2007) 'The Sacred and the Profane: The Role of Property Concepts in Disputes About Post-Mortem Examination', *Sydney Law Review* 29: 235–261.

Chapter 5

Personal jurisdiction and legal persons: the end of life

In this chapter, and Chapters 6 and 7, we extend our consideration of the relations between the authority of law and the modes of authorisation of law. In doing this, we consider jurisdiction as an activity or practice: a way of articulating (expressing) and conducting lawful relations. Chapters 6, 7 and 8 take the form of studies into how we can think with jurisdiction. In turn, each addresses a specific mode of jurisdictional practice. This chapter addresses persons, and how a jurisdiction crafts persons and personal relations. Chapter 6 looks at places, and Chapter 7 addresses events. Here, as elsewhere in this book, we are more concerned with questions that take the form 'Who?' and 'How?' rather than 'What?'. Concentrating on these questions will allow us to link the practice of jurisdiction to the substantive creation and arrangement of those lawful relations – new aspirations for law often require different forms and styles of jurisdictional practice. It also allows us to consider the forms of responsibility carried by such practices. This latter point we pick up particularly in Chapter 8.

This chapter is concerned with forms of personal jurisdiction and the law of persons. There is an extraordinarily large literature on the types, actions, characterisation, regulation and ordering of persons. Much of it is disputed. Accounts of persons are called in aid of thinking about many of the disputes about the status of the unborn, the living and the dead in relation to the wrong of abortion, the equality of men and women, and the care of the terminally ill. Persons are also invoked in the range of contrasts between nature and culture, animal and man, person and property, and so forth. The general theme of this chapter, however, is the way in which the repertoires of jurisdictional practice craft the figure of the legal person. This is rather narrower in scope than a concern with social and cultural representation of persons. It asks 'If the technical ordering of persons gives form to lawful relations, how might legal persons be understood as a part of a jurisdictional practice?'.

The jurisdictional quality of persons does not begin directly with questions of legality or illegality, nor does it begin with questions of ethical or unethical behaviour (Is it right or wrong?), rather it begins with a question of authority. Under which jurisdiction are questions of persons asked? A response to this question gives us both the source of authority, and a sense of rival authorities, for argument and dispute about the mode and manner of the configuration of lawful relations. In this chapter, we pay attention to the ways in which a jurisdictional understanding of legal persons can be viewed in terms of a repertoire of legal relations. We take as the subject matter of this chapter a jurisdictional understanding of the care of the dying. We do this to draw out the ways in which jurisdictional orderings create different ways of creating and arranging the repertoires of actions of legal persons at the end of life.

Persons and jurisdictions

Our legal language of persons is drawn from Roman, Greek and Christian understanding of persons and personality. These traditions give us a common language of law. It is possible, for example, to draw from the tradition of Roman law that the legal *persona* of Roman law is distinct from the living person.[1] This legal form gives us the status, dignities, duties and rights of the person. It also bequeaths to us the task of relating these legal forms to other forms of natural, political and ethical understanding of persons, as well as to living beings. These common sources can be traced into European theology and political philosophy and out to contemporary cultural and legal studies. Here, our analysis of the forms of personal jurisdictions brings these diverse assemblages of persons into the arrangement of jurisdictions.

Within the modern common law tradition, the jurisdiction of the regulation of dying has, at various times, been distributed between the jurisdictions of canon or ecclesiastical law, equity and that of the common law or civil government. This jurisdictional divide can be phrased in terms of a division between spiritual and temporal jurisdiction. The spiritual jurisdiction that is historically associated with the Catholic Church, and later the Church of England, is concerned loosely with conscience and spiritual life, while temporal jurisdiction is concerned with matters of civil rule and government. We discussed this in Chapter 3. In this scheme, the jurisdiction of conscience provides us with the institutional structure of the legal subject and the institutional means of achieving forms of subjectivity. The jurisdiction of government that governs relations between subjects is largely concerned with the ordering of conduct and behaviour. Modern accounts of law generally play down the role of the spiritual jurisdiction or jurisdiction of conscience in the formation of the subject. However, this has not been the case in the ordering of sacramental and private life (birth, marriage, sexual relations, death). The presence of two jurisdictions also helps us understand why so much debate about the regulation of end of life seems to be conducted in terms of rival conducts of life and existence.

Our contemporary languages of law show a marked preference for framing questions of life and death in terms of rights and persons. We worry about the quality of human rights or rights to live or to die. Here we are more concerned with the jurisdictional form of persons. The legal category of the person is one of the most important devices through which lawful relations are conducted. Thinking of the person as a legal device (or instrument) is at one level a commonplace. We are used to the consideration of the 'artificial' (i.e. legally created) personality of corporations, whether they are commercial corporations or belong to older legal forms of corporation such as the university or the Church. The modern corporation is a legal artefact and has no existence independent of its legal form. By contrast there is the category of 'natural' persons for whom the legal form is an expression (or not) of a biological life (Tur 1987). As a legal device, the corporation is used to order a range of legal relations. It also provides an important point of exchange between political, legal, social and ethical understandings of the person and personality. This is also the case with 'natural' persons, although this is rather harder to envisage. Treated as a legal device we might join legal personality to an older discussion of 'status'.

As we saw in Chapter 2, in medieval common law one jurisdictional form of organisation was status. Status can be thought of as a jurisdictional category around which rights and obligations are organised. Status was in part a matter of rank and hierarchy (Graveson 1953). In medieval law, 'status' was a jurisdictional category – law was organised and attached, for example, around one's status as a jew, a villein or a lord. One was called into court to account for breaches of obligation that arose as a result of that status. A status organised a range of dignities, honours, duties and rights. Status, we will argue, is still important to the understanding of the common law, although today its institutional and doctrinal form has been displaced by concepts such as the legal person and the laws of contract and tort. There are traces of 'status' in modern law in the concept of a minor or, as we will see, 'the terminally ill' and the rather diffuse ordering of responsibilities around 'offices'. Instead, our ordering of obligations and rights is achieved in a number of different ways. Some of these join the language of persons to the understanding of legal doctrine or to moral and political philosophy. In other situations, persons are treated as objects of social observation and subject to social inquiry and policy formation. In this section, we draw out some of the different ways in which personal jurisdiction and the category of the person continue to provide points of engagement for lawful relations. While there is an obvious sense that a personal jurisdiction is exercised in relation to persons, that relation is not always easy to delineate. In paying attention to the formulation of the authority of personal jurisdiction, we open both a question of status – the 'who' that exercises authority, and of subject – the subject of personal jurisdiction. Following on from Chapter 4, the formulation of a law of persons is treated here in terms of the consideration of technical means, that is a jurisdiction of persons is concerned with the creation and maintenance of lawful relations. The concern here is, first, with the means of establishing a legal personality or status and, second, with establishing the rights and responsibilities that attach to such a status.

We noted at the beginning of this chapter that the regulation of dying had been subject to a number of different jurisdictions and that each jurisdiction had its own account of persons and how a person relates to law and to the institutions of dying. To draw out something of the continuing importance of the jurisdictional form of persons for the regulation of the dying, we might begin with the formulation of 'dying with dignity'. To frame questions of euthanasia as ones of dignity clearly invites contest and dispute. While dignity is a generally shared language of the ethical and jurisprudential analysis of voluntary euthanasia and assisted suicide, it is not one that is uncontested (Dworkin 1993, 2011). Dignity gives us a point from which to investigate both the authority of law and the qualities or character of legal personality. We can look at the contested legal status of euthanasia and assisted suicide in terms of rival formulations of dignity: for example, dignity framed in terms of the sanctity of life (usually against any form of active assistance in dying); dignity framed in terms of autonomy or in terms of self-determination (which often frame arguments permitting assisted suicide and the right to die); and dignity framed in terms of dignified manners or civility (which frame voluntary euthanasia as the conduct of civil life and health care). The dignity which is framed as sanctity of life and as autonomy is often considered in terms of 'morality' but it can also, and more clearly, be understood by reference to the forms of jurisdiction once established by the authority of the Church and the practise of conscience. The dignity which is established through manners and civility is associated with that of the civil or temporal jurisdiction of government.

Two jurisdictions

We consider two examples that address something like a 'dignity' or 'right to die'. The first addresses dying through a civil jurisdiction, the second formulates dying in terms of a jurisdiction of conscience. Both, in a sense, assemble ways of dying well – one of dying well subject to the interests of the state or the public interest, and the other formulating dying well in terms of autonomy or conscience. Both address the question 'How might one die in a humane and dignified manner?'.[2]

Jurisdictions of civility

Over the last 30 years, there has been a major re-ordering of the civil jurisdiction over dying under medical supervision. This regulation covers the full range of the management of the end of life in hospital, including the regulation of the circumstances under which it is permissible to refuse medical treatment, the conditions that establish decision-making regimes at the end of life and the regulation of post-death care of the body. There are currently eight jurisdictions in Europe and the United States that have enacted forms of assisted suicide legislation. While no longer in force, the Australian Northern Terrritory's Rights of the Terminally Ill Act 1995 (NT) is one of a number of examples. We study it here in part because it is a discrete piece of legalisation that does not get addressed in terms of constitutional provisions and rights, and in part because the rights of the terminally ill are framed in terms of civility. This example, then, concerns the formation of a civil jurisdiction over assisted suicide and the elaboration of something like a civil status of the 'terminally ill person'.

The Rights of the Terminally Ill Act 1995 (NT) briefly permitted, in certain circumstances, a registered medical practitioner to assist a patient to 'die in a humane and dignified manner' without thereby being subject to prosecution for unlawful killing.[3] In juridical terms, this was achieved by suspending the operation of the criminal law and giving legal form to assistance in dying. The legislation was subsequently rendered ineffective by the Commonwealth in the Euthanasia Laws Act 1997 (Cth). The legislation is brief and sets out a number of rights, immunities, and administrative arrangements. In the Rights of the Terminally Ill Act 1995 (NT) s 4, confirmed a right to request assistance in dying in a dignified manner, while ss 6 and 7 set out a number of requirements that had to be fulfilled before a doctor could give assistance without criminal prosecution. What is interesting here is the range of jurisdictional devices relating to office, legal status and the administrative delimitation of role used to shape assisted suicide. The Act addressed the rights of the terminally ill along two distinct registers, one in the language of rights and the other in terms of legal immunity. The patient was represented as a petitioner before the medical practitioner and the medical practitioner was considered in relation to the Northern Territory (the state). In the Act, a patient could initiate proceedings by petitioning the medical practitioner for assistance to die in a dignified manner (s 4) by using a standard form found in Sch 7 to the Act. The relation between the doctor and the state was established by the suspension of the laws relating to unlawful killing (s 16(1)) and the establishment of an immunity from prosecution (s 20(1) and (2)).[4] If the medical practitioner had elected to assist the petitioner, then the requirements of capacity, good practice, good faith and due process set out in ss 6 and 7 would have had to be met.

The legal relations enacted in the Rights of the Terminally Ill Act 1995 (NT) did not then, as might be expected, express an ethical relation between the doctor and the patient. What bound a person to a practice of dying in a dignified manner was, rather, a series of documentary exchanges that delimit a jurisdiction (this is not to say that there could be no ethical relation between the doctor and patient but from the viewpoint of a civil jurisprudence the legal arrangements carried the weight of any ethical ordering). Central to this was the link made between the office of the medical practitioner and status of the terminally ill patient. Section 6 established the proper comportment and behaviour of the medical practitioner, and s 7 did the same for the patient. Section 6 confirmed that the medical practitioner should not be influenced by any reward or advantage, other than reasonable payment for medical services. Section 7 set out the conditions under which the medical practitioner could assist the patient. In summary terms, the medical practitioner must be satisfied that:

- the patient has the requisite capacity to decide to die in a humane and dignified manner;
- the patient is suffering from an illness that will, without extraordinary measures, lead to death, and whose only reasonable treatment is palliative with the aim of providing a comfortable death;
- the patient's illness is causing severe pain and suffering;
- all alternative treatments that might be available to the patient have been rejected;
- the patient has considered all the implications of the decision for his or her family; and
- a period of seven days has elapsed since the appropriate documentary formalities have been completed.

What is established through this array of procedural, administrative and classificatory devices is an *ars moriendi*, or preparation for death, that can be phrased in terms of an ethic and practice of civility, particularly social honour, suitable for medically assisted suicide and euthanasia. It can also be phrased in terms of a government project – whether referenced to a social domain of health or a biological or humane one of suffering (Rose and Novas 2005). It is possible to note here the various jurisdictional elements that establish this form of conduct or conduct of life. The point of jurisdictional organisation was to frame the question of assisted suicide in terms of the sovereign state ('Who can act and how?'). This frames assisted suicide as a concern of government and civil order and addresses those who occupy a number of roles (offices): citizen, patient, medical practitioner, social worker, and so on. However, it is also possible to draw out the sense in which this legislation responds on an older form of jurisdiction – that of chivalry, which was concerned with matters of honour and dignity (see Chapter 4). It draws attention to the ways in which questions of dignity and honour belong to the realm of public appearance and relationship. Dignity here is bound to status and so too the person.

A second point of jurisdictional ordering concerns the status of the 'terminally ill patient'. The status established by the legislation is hardly classical in form. It did not refer to a tenurial relation or to an office. It had only limited legal effect and its conditions of assumption were voluntary. However, in other respects it was typical of a common law legal status: it did not address the whole legal person so much as make a status out of an exception to the (natural) legal person (Graveson 1953: 5). In doing this, it might be analogised to the status of a child at common law. It is possible to follow the jurisdictional shaping of the terminally ill person further through the legislation – the form of the legislation establishes the repertoires of conduct for the staging of medically assisted suicide. First, someone making a request would have needed to show a demonstrable capacity to understand the purpose of killing oneself in social, ethical and clinical terms. Second, they would have had to possess a set of competencies in the management of one's affairs in relation to kin. Third, it was necessary to master the protocols of self-administered suicide. Framing such actions in terms of a jurisdictional practice draws attention to the capacity required to conduct ethical arguments, and the ability to direct regulatory practices to carry out identifiable procedures and achieve particular ends. The emphasis of manners and civility in the performance of role established the conduct necessary to sustain a status within an institutional and ethical milieu (Minson 1993: 37).

There is no doubt that this is an impoverished description of dying in a humane and dignified manner. However, this in itself should be no surprise. In descriptive terms the Rights of the Terminally Ill Act 1995 (NT) was primarily concerned with establishing the legal conditions of the conduct of dying under medical supervision. More prosaically, the Act was only one source of information about the appropriate conduct of doctors, patients and the state. Other sources of guidance as to conduct might be found in the documentation of the practice of palliative care, professional ethics, and choices of the patient and their kin. However, this description of the regulation that permits dying in a dignified manner is 'thin' for another reason: the performance of dying well is studiously left out of the governmental account, as is the role of the doctor, whether as health care provider or judge. These questions are met by the consent procedures.

So far we have traced the jurisdictional form of the 'terminally ill person'. It was also necessary for the legislation to delimit the scope of the civil jurisdiction. Assisted suicide under medical supervision had to be accommodated within the general regulation of the protection of the lives of citizens. The Rights of the Terminally Ill Act 1995 (NT) accommodated dying in a humane and dignified manner in relation to the jurisdiction of criminal law by pursuing three approaches. First, by stating that a doctor would commit no crime. Acting within the authority of the legislation would be considered a medical treatment. Second, that any death need not be reported to the coroner as unnatural. Third, that a medical practitioner would be granted immunity from prosecution if a death complied with the terms of the legislation. In jurisdictional terms, then, the status of the terminally ill person was given meaning by creating a domain of law apart from the criminal law. Assisted suicide was to be considered a medical treatment, but the relation between medical treatment and criminal law was suspended.

Viewed as an action of civil jurisdiction, the suspension of the address of law can be considered in two aspects: first, in terms of the pluralisation of jurisdiction over dying under medical supervision; and second, in terms of the audience of law. In relation to the former, it can be noted that the suspension of laws continued both to maintain the jurisdictional authority of law in relation to other discourses of homicide and other practices of suicide and euthanasia. In the Rights of the Terminally Ill Act 1995 (NT), state law was represented as being subordinate neither to a higher ethical law – for example, the ethic of relieving suffering or of medical necessity – nor to an administrative regime that departs fully from legal normativity. The form of rights represented in the Act was also specific to a particular jurisdiction. The Act did not make statements of general rights (natural, human or constitutional), but established a specific set of rights and immunities within a legal administrative structure. It proceeded, that is, by attributing a specific status (the terminally ill patient in unbearable pain) for a particular purpose (dying in a dignified manner), rather than by elaborating a general status (the bearer of human rights or subjectivity). It can be argued that the legislation has not simply confirmed the rights of the terminally ill but created, or has joined, a new jurisdiction concerning the care of dying.

In this section, we have followed the work of civil jurisdiction in establishing a legal domain for providing medical assistance in dying in a dignified manner. It has been narrated as part of a jurisdiction over persons – even though the work of civil authority makes it hard not to view it in terms of the interests of the management of civil authority and of the management of population within a territorial jurisdiction. The analysis of the Rights of the Terminally Ill Act 1995 (NT) presented here has drawn out the ways in which a contemporary jurisdiction over dying in a dignified manner might be understood as a continuing form of personal jurisdiction. At the centre of the civil understanding of dying in a dignified manner were a number of technical jurisdictional delimitations of status and action. The subject matter of this jurisdiction is the repertoire of actions available to a 'terminally ill' person. The claim of a civil jurisprudence is that it is still possible to reason within law about the concerns of dignity, civility and social health. The technologies of a civil jurisdiction have been used to create a specific way of dying.

Jurisdictions of conscience

In our second example, we turn attention to the jurisdiction of conscience. Since the disarticulation of the jurisdictions of civility and conscience in the 17th century, it is difficult to formulate any simple question of authority and jurisdiction of conscience that is not expressed in terms of a rivalry of jurisdictions. Chapter 3 set out the ways in which the common law was formed internally around the enfolding of rival jurisdictions into forms of sovereign territorial jurisdiction. However, questions of conscience and the appropriate form of subjectivity continue to dominate much critical thinking about law. Here we provide another way of thinking about the status and conduct of the terminally ill. The forms of dignity within this jurisdiction are associated with human beings and humanity, rather than the dignity that is associated with rank, office, and role. The dignity of conscience crosses without much translation, into the domains

of moral philosophy and practical reason concerned with the acknowledgement of the sacredness or sanctity of life. However, the jurisdiction
of conscience does not join so readily with civil forms of jurisdictional
practice.

In what follows, we briefly consider the form of the legal person in
Washington v Glucksberg 521 US 702. *Washington v Glucksberg*, along
with another case heard at the same time – *Vacco v Quill* 521 US 793
(1997) – decided that it was not unconstitutional to treat assisted suicide
as a criminal act. In these cases, a number of doctors and patients
challenged the constitutionality of laws that made assisted suicide a
criminal office. In *Quill*, it was argued that since it was lawful for
a competent adult to refuse medical treatment it was unconstitutional to
ban assisted suicide under medical supervision as there was no essential
difference between terminating treatment and administering lethal drugs.
To decide otherwise, it was argued, would violate the 14th Amendment
– the equal protection clause – because it would prevent some people
from making decisions about the end of their lives.[5] It would be
unconstitutional, they argued, to ban medically assisted suicide for those
not able to assist themselves when termination of medical treatment
was permitted for others. It would mean that there was not equal treatment of the terminally ill. In *Glucksberg*, the argument was phrased in
terms of liberty and the violation of the due process clause of the 14th
Amendment. There it was argued that there was a liberty interest in
managing the time of death. Both cases succeeded in the lower courts.
However, the Supreme Court determined that a prohibition on assisted
suicide could be constitutional. It is the *Glucksberg* decision that we
follow here because it raises most clearly the relation between conscience
and form of legal persons.

How does the court consider a jurisdiction of the person? At first
glance, the decision in *Glucksberg* does not concern itself so much with
the question of who or what is a legal person or a person dying before the
law. Rather, the court preferred to ask questions about the scope and
method of the due process clause. However, following the kinds of
analysis we presented in Chapter 3, we might look at due process in terms
of a jurisdictional practice. What is created through such a technique is
not directed to civil authority and government as such, but to the
formation and ordering of a conscience – in this case a form of liberty.
This sounds odd if such concerns are viewed from a critical perspective
of overcoming authority and law in the name of liberty, but this is not the
task of the court in this case. The court is concerned to align liberty and
conscience with jurisdiction and the authority of law. The decision can be

viewed as a series of techniques – due processes – for shaping liberty. In modern law, we have inherited a variety of different and rival jurisdictional forms through which to create conscience and freedom. Here we follow the arguments of Rehnquist CJ and Stevens J and then turn to the work of the jurisprudent Ronald Dworkin. Dworkin directs attention away from liberty and freedom toward a concern with dignity – not the dignity of rank and manners, however, but the dignity of respect for the human being.

For Rehnquist CJ, due process cases must begin 'by examining our Nation's history, legal traditions, and practices' (at 710). This involves an examination of the history of the prohibition against suicide, which he traces to the ecclesiastical jurisdiction as far back as 673 AC (at 711). Rehnquist CJ refers also to early common law prohibitions (at 711–712), but what is interesting about these is that they are framed in terms of felony (it is a felony to try to kill oneself) and of forfeiture (if you succeed, your property is forfeit to the crown), rather than in terms of conscience. It is not until at least the 16th century that we see the common law taking the position that this is a most horrid crime against God and Nature (*Hales v Petit*, 1 Plowd Com 253, 261, 75 Eng Rep 387, 400 (1561–1562), cited at 712). However, what is protected by the due process clause is liberty. Thus, in the judgment, arguments about conscience, liberty and rights are held in place as common law arguments about crime and property. For Rehnquist, the question is one of law, not philosophy, so the answer to whether it is constitutional to treat assisted suicide as murder must be given jurisdictional authority within the common law (at 727). Liberty of conscience, it seems, belongs to the common law.

Stevens J, on the other hand, gives us a natural jurisdiction of liberty. He notes that the 'basic concept of freedom . . . is even older than the common law' (at 743). His account of due process is part of a training in keeping that natural freedom alive. Citing the earlier case of *Cruzan v Director Missouri Department of Health* (491 US 110), he further notes that the right to refuse medical treatment 'rests not simply on the common-law right to refuse medical treatment, but, – at least implicitly – , on the even more fundamental right to make this "deeply personal decision"' (at 744). Thus, Stevens' account of due process is linked to dignity, autonomy and conscience. While Rehnquist tries to hold onto a common law jurisdiction, albeit one which folds in questions of conscience, Stevens J formulates his decision within a jurisdiction of natural order – of natural liberty.

One of the problems of seeing the jurisdiction of the person here is that in modern law there is almost always an overlay of other modes of jurisdiction. Here, the ways in which the various arguments are structured around the person are obscured to some extent by the need to weigh individual liberty against state interests. However, the reiteration of state interests should not hide the way in which the decisions are shaped around a jurisdiction of individual liberty and conscience.

Further, the due process clause generally can be thought of as a jurisdictional device. It gives us ways of creating lawful relations. One way of thinking about differences between the judgments in *Glucksberg* concerning the interpretation of the due process clause would be to consider them in terms of the ordering of authority and the arrangement of legal relations. In Chapter 3, we considered a number of technologies of jurisdiction, including the ways in which precedent binds persons to law. For Rehnquist CJ in due process cases it is imperative to carefully enumerate the liberty interests. 'Liberty' interests have been, he says, 'carefully refined by concrete examples involving fundamental rights found to be deeply rooted in our legal tradition' (at 722). The right in which the respondents are interested is freedom from government interference in end of life decisions (at 724). The right to direct the removal of life sustaining medical treatment, Rehnquist CJ notes, 'was not simply deduced from abstract concepts of personal autonomy . . . The decision was entirely consistent with this nation's history and con-stitutional traditions' (at 725). For Rehnquist, then, the question is what gets bound to low? Or, perhaps, what does the binding to law? It seems that for him it is the nation's history and traditions. So while it appears that initially for Rehnquist the answer to whether it is constitutional to treat assisted suicide as murder must be framed in terms of common law technicality – the answer must be found within the common law – in the end it is rather the conscience and values of the nation which bind persons to law. It is less easy, however, to see what Stevens J binds to law. One of the problems with his judgment is that having recognised a natural jurisdiction of liberty, he then agrees that state interests in this case override that liberty. He simply binds the person to the interests of the state, but leaves the conscience of the person free – for now. The difficulty that needs to be addressed, therefore, is how to find a legal technique which makes sense of arguments of jurisdiction of the person.

In *Glucksberg* and *Vacco* we have seen the Supreme Court viewing the legal person as a concern of both a jurisdiction of civility and of conscience. Ultimately, for the court assisted suicide was treated as a matter of civil jurisdiction. Our final comments turn, therefore, to an account of a jurisdiction of conscience not subordinate to the civil authority of the state but instead figured in terms of rights. Although there are many writers who address the question of rights and the right to die and live, our example is taken from the work of Ronald Dworkin (Dworkin 1993, 2011). In his book, *Life's Dominion*, Dworkin engages with the constitutional understanding of the status of assisted suicide and abortion. In such matters of life and death, Dworkin argues, we are concerned with the formulation of our most profound religious and ethical beliefs. He wants to draw the concern with liberty and conscience into law in 'matters involving the most intimate and personal choices a person may make in a lifetime, choices central to personal dignity and autonomy' (*Planned Parenthood v Casey*, 505 US 833, 851). As a jurisprudent, unlike the Supreme Court, he offers a way of linking the moral, religious and political understanding of assisted suicide. Dworkin is interested in showing that despite intense disputes about the status and value of abortion and assisted suicide, there is a rational and principled way of deliberating about the intrinsic value of the sanctity or the sacredness of life or, in the language we have been using, of dignity (Dworkin 2011). For Dworkin, if people are prepared to acknowledge that they are engaged in disputing a common concept with respect – the sanctity or sacredness of life – then there are means of weighing the value of rival conceptions. In this account due process, and the integrity of due process, is one part of the means by which we engage our common response to the profound questions of human life. Dworkin's account of dominion or jurisdiction is one of reason shaped around a concern with the intrinsic importance of human life (Dworkin 1993: 236). It is a jurisdiction of truth and of conscience. Dworkin is not simply concerned with formal reasoning since, for him, such arguments directly shape, and reflect on, the possibilities of living and dying well. These concerns all form a part of his understanding of the person and legal person. For Dworkin, the rights associated with assistance with dying should be shaped around the requirement that people never be treated in a way that denies the distinct importance of their own life.

However, if we take personal jurisdiction as involved in the creation of relations and personal relations, then we see more clearly some of the jurisdictional tasks that are being formed. We can, of course, worry about whether they are appropriate or adequate to the task or, more critically, whether the task is indeed one worth achieving. At this point, juris-dictional thinking joins with a broader range of concerns to do with the formation of the modern legal subject. Dworkin's argument fixes attention on dignity and on intrinsic worth. We can consider this a modern version of a religious jurisdiction. While there is an engagement with law and 'the right to die', the language of the sanctity of life and autonomy focuses on the ways in which dignity is shaped around the obligation or duty to live well. Legal forms are there to assist in this matter. Whether or not we would want to associate this as belonging to a religious conduct of life is open to dispute. Dworkin rightly asserts that this is not his concern (MacNeil 2007).

Persons who die

We have presented here a number of accounts of personal jurisdiction. Our task has been to make visible the continuing work of personal jurisdiction. We have investigated ways in which forms of jurisdictional practice have shaped and created legal relations. In the first part of the chapter we looked at how a law of persons – and forms of dignity – were shaped according to two or more jurisdictional practices. We emphasised there the difference jurisdictional form makes to the framing of questions of persons by showing the ways in which it is possible to understand dignity in dying or in medically assisted suicide. In doing this, we also showed some of the ways in which the techniques of the ordering of legal relations might be considered in terms of a jurisdictional practice of the making of legal persons. At one level this can be understood in terms of the repertoires of legal action made available. Legislation like the Rights of the Terminally Ill Act 1997 (NT) or the Washington Death with Dignity Act (RCW 70.245 (in force since 2009)) give legal form to assisted suicide. However, we argued that it did so by drawing on an understanding of the relations and forms of law of a civil jurisdiction (and rather speculatively as an echo of a jurisdiction of chivalry). What is bound to law is a series of public actions, social tasks and attributes. These are held and organised around the civil status of the terminally ill person. In the civil jurisdiction, there is very little that needs to be said about the inner life of conscience because the civil jurisdiction is ordered around a concern with manners and action.

In the second part of the chapter, discussing the decision in *Glucksberg*, we saw a more complex formulation of the relations between the jurisdictions of conscience and civility. The concerns of the case are pre-eminently phrased in terms of liberty and freedom. This might look like a matter of conscience, but in the end conscience is subordinated to the interests of state. As a result, what is dispositive is the relation of the dying person to the public interest of civil authority (the state). The legal person of *Glucksberg* is shaped in relation to the nation (Rehnquist CJ) or by a relation to ancient liberty (Stevens J). What is at issue in these judgments is made clearer by Dworkin's unequivocal formulation of the dignified person of conscience. To die in Ronald Dworkin's jurisdiction of conscience requires considerable philosophical engagement and reflection. It requires or encourages an inner personality capable of reflecting on, and reasoning about, dignity, autonomy or the sacredness of life. In the jurisdiction of conscience, it is not civil authority and manners that is paramount, but conscience – whether it be individual conscience or the collective conscience of the political or ethical community.

Conclusion

In this chapter, in following the jurisdictional formation of legal persons, we have developed the account of legal form and authority in two ways. First, we have deepened the account of the form of law by linking the formation of legal persons to the practice of jurisdictions. Second, we have begun to point towards some of the different forms of jurisdictional practices in relation to persons. Our analysis has shown a number of ways in which the regulation of dying under medical supervision, or assisted suicide, or equal treatment, draws on different jurisdictional forms. Not only is the legal person a *persona* or mask, it is one that operates as a jurisdictional device, creating and ordering legal relations. In emphasising the jurisdictional form of persons, it is possible to engage more clearly with the sense in which legal form continues to shape human relations (at the end of life). It is also possible to see the way in which legal form – understood as a practice – shapes the authority of law. Attending to the jurisdictional variety of the regulation of the end of life also complicates the ways in which we might understand authority and the authorisation of law. To view such regulation simply as an act of sovereign will or reason is to impose more uniformity than is present in legal practice. It also deflects attention from the material and institutional ordering of law and of dying under medical supervision.

Finally, the linking of authority and the jurisdictional form of the legal person raises questions of the responsibility of the jurisprudent and the critic. The office of jurisprudent (and judge) is also placed in relation to jurisdiction. As our reading of Dworkin shows, our contemporary mixing of jurisdictions, and the comparative lack of institutional shaping of jurisdictions of conscience, mean that most institutional understanding of law tends to be operated through the jurisdictions of civil authority. A jurisprudent has to be able to address the reality of jurisdictional forms as well as consider their limits and transformation. Where critical and transformative engagements with law rest on jurisdictions of conscience, it is difficult to gain purchase on the jurisdictional forms that might be appropriate to the task. This concern is felt acutely in those projects that attempt to bring substantive forms of identity or subjecthood into relation with domains of law: the raced, gendered and sexed person is yet to enter the domain of common law in any material way (Davies 2008).

This position is even more pointed when critical accounts of law seek to address or create *personae* that are set outside the orthodox repertoire of legal actors (say, for example, the nomad, the gypsy, the animal, the Marrano or the environment). Here, the wager of new forms of personality and conducts of life is that it is both possible to articulate new forms of conduct and that there are patterns of lawful relations to be established.

Notes

1   The literature on persons is extensive: Burchell draws out the links between *persona* and the formation of public office (Burchell 1998); Hunter and Saunders provide an outline of the important work of the sociologist Marcel Mauss (Hunter and Saunders 1995); Mussawir offers an account of the legal person in terms of the plurality of legal forms (Mussawir 2011: ch 2); and Parsley offers an account of the theatrical form of the person (Parsley 2010).
2   For a more detailed consideration of this matter, see McVeigh 2007.
3   The terminology of 'dying in a humane and dignified manner' is taken from Rights of the Terminally Ill Act 1995 (NT), Sch 7.
4   Section 16(1), states that: 'Notwithstanding the Northern Territory Criminal Code, s 26(3), an action taken in accordance with this Act by a medical practitioner or by a health care provider on the instructions of a medical practitioner does not constitute an offence against Part VI of the Code or an attempt to commit such an offence, a conspiracy to commit such an offence, or an offence of aiding, abetting, counselling or procuring the commission of such an offence.
    The Northern Territory Criminal Code, s 26(3) states: 'A person cannot authorize or permit another to kill him or, except in the case of medical treatment, to cause him grievous harm'. The Northern Territory Criminal Code, Part VI deals with offences against the person and other matters. Division 1 of Part VI outlines duties relating to the preservation of human life. A death that had occurred in accordance with the Rights of the Terminally Ill Act 1995 (NT) would not be in breach of a duty to preserve human life, but it would have remained the case that this death was not authorised or permitted by the deceased'.
5   The 14th Amendment provides that: 'All persons born or naturalized in the United States, and subject to the jurisdiction thereof, are citizens of the United States and of the state wherein they reside. No state shall make or enforce any law which shall abridge the privileges or immunities of citizens of the United States; nor shall any state deprive any person of life, liberty, or property, without due process of law; nor deny to any person within its jurisdiction the equal protection of the laws'.

References

Burchell, D. (1998) 'Civic Personae: MacIntyre, Cicero and Moral Personality', *History of Political Thought* 19: 101–118.

Davies, M. (2008) *Asking the Law Question*, 3rd edn, Sydney: Law Book Company.

Dworkin, R. (1993) *Life's Dominion: An Argument about Abortion and Euthanasia, and Individual Theory*, London: Harper Collins.

Dworkin, R. (2011) *Justice for Hedgehogs*, Cambridge, MA: Belknap Press.

Graveson, R. (1953) *Status in the Common Law*, London: Athlone Press.

Hunter, I. and Saunders, D. (1995) 'Walks of Life: Mauss on the Human Gymnasium', *Body and Society* 1(2): 65–81.

MacNeil, W.P. (2007) *Lex Populi: The Jurisprudence of Popular Culture*, Stanford, CA: Stanford University Press.

McVeigh, S. (2007) 'Subjects of Jurisdiction: The Dying, Northern Territory, Australia, 1995–1997', in McVeigh, S. (ed), *Jurisprudence of Jurisdiction*, London: Routledge.

Minson, J. (1993) *Questions of Conduct*, London: Macmillan.

Mussawir, E. (2011) *Jurisdiction in Deleuze: The Expression and Representation of Law*, Abingdon: Routledge-Cavendish.

Parsley, C. (2010) 'The Mask and Agamben: the Transitional Juridical Technics of Legal Relation', *Law Text Culture*, 14(1): 12–39.

Rose, N. and Novas, C. (2005) 'Biological Citizenship', in Ong, A. and Collier, S. (eds), *Global Assemblages: Technologies, Politics, and Ethics as Anthropological Problems*, Oxford: Blackwell.

Tur, R. (1987) 'The "Person" in Law', in Peacocke, A. and Gillett, G. (eds), *Persons and Personality: A Contemporary Inquiry*, Oxford: Blackwell.

Chapter 6

Jurisdictional encounters and the meeting of laws

Any critical approach to law must engage with the effects and affects of sovereign territorial jurisdictions on an understanding of the engagement of lawful relations, In this chapter we think of legal place as a practice of jurisdiction. Place is not, as might be thought, a matter of legally bounded physical space, but rather it is the work of legal ordering and relationship. Jurisdictional practices create legal places through engaging with the material world. The jurisdictional form of the sovereign territorial state creates relations of place (in fact many) but as we saw in Chapter 3 these are not the only jurisdictional ways of creating places. In this chapter we approach jurisdictions of place by looking at the meeting of laws. We do so because it gives us a privileged and local site of lawful place-making. It allows us to talk about the particular ways in which the jurisprudences of jurisdiction create relations of place. This task could be huge since all laws – not just laws of war and laws of property and planning – address place. Here, however, we concentrate on the meeting of indigenous and non-indigenous jurisdictions in Australia. We do so to draw out the sense of the meeting of jurisdictions and the making of legal places are both a matter of technical ordering and of the conduct of lawful relations. To do this, we look at the meeting of common law and indigenous jurisdictions, first in the 19th century as a concern of personal jurisdiction, and then in the 20th century as a concern of territorial jurisdiction. From there we draw our concerns back into the quality of the meeting places of common law.

There are three important considerations to be addressed in formulating the meeting of laws from the perspective of jurisdiction: first, 'Where are the meeting places of law?'; second, 'What law is brought to the meeting?'; and, third, 'How is the meeting of laws conducted?'. Where laws meet is not always clear. The contemporary regimes of international law imagine laws as framed around sovereign territorial states. For some, the territorial arrangements of sovereign states are held in place by their recognition in the international legal order. For others, it is the assertion of territorial sovereignty that places states in the international order. In either case, it is necessary to negotiate, align, or re-assemble those jurisdictions of law that do not conform to this representation. Typically in the doctrinal ordering of law, we divide these concerns between international, national and customary legal orders, and devise complex rules to negotiate relations between them. In this chapter, however, we hold the place of law around discrete forms of jurisdictional practice and the jurisdictional practice of the meeting of laws.

In considering the way law gives place in terms of jurisdiction, as in previous chapters we address the broad inheritance of forms of juris-diction in terms of the jurisdictions of conscience and civility. In a modern idiom, we argue, a meeting of sovereign territorial jurisdictions can be imagined in terms of a jurisdiction of civility. Its treaties of amity or relations of enmity would be framed in terms of sovereign civil authority. This is a crude characterisation of the international relations imagined by European public law in the 17th and 18th centuries. Another example of the meeting of jurisdictions might be found in the area of conflict of laws (sometimes known as private international law). There a body of law has been developed to determine choice of law and choice of forum between parties. These examples both presuppose an estab-lished meeting of jurisdictions and agree the terms on which the meeting is taking place. International law is traditionally a law between sovereign states, while conflict of laws concerns relations between established and known jurisdictions. By contrast, in this chapter, in order to draw out something of the character of practice of a sovereign territorial juris-diction, attention is paid to a form of jurisdictional engagement in which there is no prior agreement – or, more strongly, there is an active dispute as to the authority and existence of another law or jurisdiction. Here, we look at the way in which the contemporary focus on territorial jurisdiction has often rendered indigenous jurisdictions invisible to common law. For many critics in such situations it is more appropriate to draw on the resources of a jurisdiction of conscience to enable a meeting place of law. Within such a jurisdiction a meeting place might be imagined, with difficulty, in terms of the acknowledgement of common humanity or of a shared understanding of, or ambition for, just relations. In this chapter, we take the specific example of the meeting of indigenous and common laws to examine the ways in which jurisdictional practices of place have been put to use.

Territorial jurisdiction

One way of seeing where laws meet is through the encounter of the common law and imperial law with other legal orders beyond England, in particular those of indigenous authority in the former colonies of the British Empire. The encounter between the common law and other laws or jurisdictions took place in different times, places and ways across the globe. Like the legal ordering of England, the ordering of British colonisation was largely an affair of jurisdiction. It was through jurisdiction that the authority of the common law was asserted and that the legal settlement of the plantations and colonies was originally effected. That post-colonising and post-colonial settlements have increasingly turned to constitutional orders (for example, Constitution Act, s 35 (Canada), which protects 'existing aboriginal rights') upon which to found their nations only re-institutes the conceptual ordering of state-sovereign-territory that dominates modernity – and obscures the continuing dispossession of law and land in decolonisation. In order to see this work of common law jurisdiction more clearly, we use the example of the recognition of native title – indigenous rights to land – in Australia. What makes this a particularly powerful example is that, unlike Canada, or even the United States, Australia has not yet turned to constitutionalism to define the relationship of the Australian nation to its indigenous inhabitants. The Australian situation shows most clearly the way in which thinking about legal ordering and engagement with law through sovereignty obscures the meeting of peoples and the laws they follow – of the meeting of common law and indigenous law – as a jurisdictional practice. (It also shows the ways in which questions of conscience have no easy jurisdictional form.)

In the 19th century, it was relatively easy to see the relationship between indigenous and non-indigenous as a jurisdictional concern of civil authority. Prior to the 1830s, the ordering of New South Wales was considered a matter of jurisdiction. Judges understood that while sovereignty had been claimed over a large proportion of the East of Australia, the Crown had little effective control over that area. In effect, the British had an inchoate title, subject to possession. Effective control and common law jurisdiction was restricted to an area within the limits of settlement around Sydney. Jurisdiction was asserted largely on the basis of a person's status, not on the basis of territory. The settlers were under the control of the common law by the birthright principle: as Englishmen (sic) they carried as much of the law as was applicable to the circumstances of the colony. It was not until 1824 that it was confirmed that settlers were amenable to English law for violence against the Aborigines (*R v Lowe* (1827) NSWKR 4). Conversely, while Aborigines were amenable to English law for violence against settlers, it was held that they were not under the jurisdiction of the common law for crimes against each other. Even when the British government gave territorial jurisdiction to the Supreme Court of New South Wales in 1828 (Australian Courts Act (1828) 9 Geo IV c 83), that jurisdiction only applied to settlers (*R v Ballard or Barrett* (1829) NSWSupC 26), leaving Aboriginal Australians beyond the writ of the common law. In this period, therefore, the predominant mode of jurisdiction was that of status – the common law applied to settlers because of their status as subjects (and later because they were within British territory) – while it did not apply to indigenous Australians precisely because they were not yet considered to be subjects. While they were under the 'protection' of the common law, that did not extend to subjecthood. When it is finally determined in 1836, in a case called *Murrell*, that Aborigines are amenable to English law in all circumstances, an important plank in the reasoning was a decision that the British crown had now effectively asserted territorial jurisdiction in a more modern sense – over all within the territory (*R v Murrell and Bummaree* (1836) 1 Legge 72). Despite *Murrell*, and echoing the continuing plurality of laws of England, it was common until the 1860s for barristers to commence proceedings involving Aboriginal defendants with a plea to the jurisdiction of the court: effectively, a claim that another law applied.

While it is relatively easy to see the ordering of legal relations in colonial times as a matter of jurisdiction, it is less easy to see this in modern law. In part, this is because of the shift in conceptual language in the 20th century from that of jurisdiction to that of sovereignty – and in particular because of the now dominance of territorial jurisdiction, allied to the sovereign nation state. Legal relations are created through the sovereign of the territorial state, and not, say, a relation of persons. This is most obvious in native title decisions in Australia – particularly the key decisions of the High Court of Australia in *Mabo v State of Queensland (No 2)* (1992) 175 CLR 1 and *Members of the Yorta Yorta Community v Victoria* (2002) 194 ALR 538. As will be seen, the instantiation of territorial sovereignty in these cases has had the effect of making it difficult to discern where in modern law the meeting point between jurisdictions might be and what a meeting place might require.

In 1992 in *Mabo (No 2)*, the High Court of Australia began to discuss what it considered as the legal fact of the continuing existence of indigenous interests in land in the form of an interest named native title.

This interest, the High Court asserted, was founded in the relationship of indigenous Australians to their country and survived the annexation of the continent and the establishment of sovereignty by Great Britain. This recognition, however, caused a problem for the court. On the one hand, the majority held that native title was sourced in the laws, customs and traditions of Aboriginal Australians. On the other, the court was unwilling to accord any contemporary authority to indigenous laws and jurisdiction. How then is the meeting of common law and indigenous jurisdictions to be understood by those living within a common law tradition (Rush 1997a, 1997b)?

According to the High Court, all rights and recognition flow from the moment of assertion of sovereignty, although the acquisition of sovereignty itself is non-justiciable before the court. In particular, the assertion of sovereignty has the important consequence that at the moment of acquisition the common law became the law of the land, and of the territory. This is, in a precise sense, an assertion of civil authority. While it is presented in relation to indigenous laws and jurisdictions, it is also an assertion that the High Court does not speak in the form of a jurisdiction of conscience. Justice is to be understood as a technique of civil ordering and conduct. According to Brennan J, in a settled colony (a colony that was legally considered 'desert and uninhabited'), such as Australia, the colonists bring with them 'as much of English law as [was] applicable to their own situation and the condition of an infant colony' (*Mabo (No 2)*, at 35). But, according to Brennan J, the law of England was not merely the personal law of the English colonists – it became the law of the land – of not just Europeans, but of indigenous Australian (*Mabo (No 2)*, at 37). In Brennan J's versions of events, sovereignty was acquired over the territory of the eastern part of Australia, and the common law became the law of the territory and of the land. The description of sovereignty offered by the High Court, and Brennan J in particular, is orthodox: sovereignty is co-extensive with the modern state, and indivisible – the entire power of the state has to be vested in a single locus, a centralised legal authority. There is one law of the land and the nation. It is a description of the so-called post-Westphalian international legal order described in Chapter 3.

Mabo (No 2) was followed a few years later by the decision in *Yorta Yorta*. While in *Mabo (No 2)* we see the importance of territorial jurisdiction in effacing other forms of legal ordering (other jurisdictions), the key to this latter case was the tying of territorial sovereignty to a single national law. Just as in *Mabo (No 2)* the key point of departure for thinking about native title lay, and continues to lie, with the assertion of sovereignty by the British Crown, in *Yorta Yorta* the narrative of sovereignty was presented in stark terms. The assertion of sovereignty by the British Crown 'necessarily entailed' that thereafter there could be 'no parallel law-making system in the territory over which it asserted sovereignty. To hold otherwise would be to deny the acquisition of sovereignty and . . . that is not permissible' (*Yorta Yorta*, at 552). The logic of state sovereignty requires this:

> Upon the Crown acquiring sovereignty, the normative or law-making system which then existed could not thereafter validly create new rights, duties or interests. Rights or interests in land created after sovereignty and which owed their origin and continued existence *only* to a normative system other than that of the new sovereign power, would not and will not be given effect by the legal order of the new sovereign.
>
> (*Yorta Yorta*, at 552)

Thus, for the majority there is an inevitable link, or a 'necessary entailment', between sovereignty, legal system and territory. The status of this 'necessary entailment' is not easy to establish. On the one hand, it might be a statement of law, albeit one that is made without reference to any direct authority. On the other hand, the claim could be understood as being of a logical or axiomatic nature. The assertion of sovereignty, and the authority of law, it might be thought from the above, can only be accomplished in terms of an absolute (legal) occupation/dominion of a territory. Sovereignty is a matter of authority, and of submission to authority, and it is inextricably linked to territory.

One of the effects of territorial sovereignty being the dominant mode of jurisdiction in modern law is that it makes it more difficult to see other jurisdictions, including those of indigenous Australians. It is the re-alignment of territorial sovereignty with the Australian nation as a result of *Mabo (No 2)* and, in particular *Yorta Yorta*, which stops us from seeing any other mode of jurisdictional engagement between laws. Yet in the 19th century, prior to the establishment of territorial jurisdiction, as can be seen from the brief paragraph above, legal relations were ordered through a different mode of jurisdiction – namely that of status. Prior to the recognition of territorial sovereignty in *Murrell*, jurisdiction was asserted over both indigenous Australians and settlers by virtue of their status – either as British subjects or not. Even after *Murrell*, it was not a foregone conclusion that territorial sovereignty would necessarily render all within it only subject to British law. As we have previously discussed, including in Chapter 5, jurisdiction based on status (or personal jurisdiction) still exists in modern law, but is often subordinated to the jurisdiction of the state.

One of the political attractions of thinking about the relations between indigenous and non-indigenous peoples and laws through the lens of territorial sovereignty has been that it reduced the need to think about where the meeting point of laws might be. In part, this is so because we assume that the meeting point of laws is ordered in terms of the meeting of sovereign territorial states. If this is so then there is according to common law no real meeting of common law and indigenous law. Alternatively – and this has been central to British colonisation, there is a meeting point but it is not exactly a meeting of laws, it is a meeting of common law and something less than law – custom or culture (Dorsett and McVeigh 2005). While territory might be considered a poor meeting place, because it has left no room for the acknowledgement of indigenous law and jurisdiction, it is a simple one – law bound to defined space leaves little room for the authority of any other than that law to be recognised. This does not mean that territorial jurisdiction has ended indigenous jurisdictions. It does mean, however, that the conditions of the meeting have been set in terms that have rendered the meeting of laws one-sided and often meaningless.

The argument above has been presented in terms of the conditions of the meeting of law established through two different jurisdictional orders. It should be noted, as it was in *Mabo (No 2)*, that what this meeting involved was an imposition of the English common law and the consequent displacement of indigenous laws and dispossession of indigenous peoples. To consider place in terms of a practice of jurisdiction, then, is to consider it in terms of the quality of a series of jurisdictional relationships. Next, we turn to some of the detail of the creation and maintenance of the points of engagements of law within the Australian common law. In the way that we have addressed jurisdiction, the meeting points of law are maintained through the technologies of law. In following the meeting of common law and indigenous jurisdictions, we return to the technologies of jurisdiction and the practices of mapping and the naming of legal relations discussed in Chapter 3.

Two technologies

Picture three images, all of a native title claim area. The first is a map of the claim area, demarcated by latitude and longitude. The areas that cannot be claimed are marked with hatching. There are crown reservation numbers, and a scale in kilometres – in fact, all the things we expect in a tenure map. The other two images are paintings on canvas, in a form that Westerners have labelled 'dot painting'. Yet all three address similar concerns, albeit expressed through different cultural lenses: in Western legal terms, jurisdiction, territory and ownership; for the Pila Nguru – the creators of the painting – the Tjukurrpa.[1]

In 1995, the Spinifex people lodged a native title claim with the Native Title Tribunal. As part of the native title process, an art project was established to record and document ownership of the Spinifex area. Two paintings were produced initially, one painted by the men and one by the women (Cane 2002: 16–17). These are described as 'native title paintings'. In 1998, the Spinifex people entered into a framework agreement with the Western Australian government, which was ratified by Parliament. The paintings were formally included in the preamble of the agreement (Cane 2002: 16). For the Spinifex people, the paintings are part of mapping territory.[2]

As we discussed in Chapter 3, mapping creates and makes legal relations visible. Maps are a creation and visible representation of authority, evidencing a movement of a jurisdiction and a law across land, between humans and events. Here, we want to concentrate on mapping as part of the practice of lawful relations. In this example, we follow the practices of mapping in establishing or representing the jurisdictional engagement of non-indigenous and indigenous jurisdictions in Australia. If we remind ourselves that as a technology, mapping works towards the crafting of a jurisdiction, then we need to consider what form of legal relations it engages. At one level, mapping engages legal relations through its representation of particular political or legal forms of the sovereign territorial state. It is the representation of political or legal form, and in particular of the modern territorial state, which engages people, places and events and creates lawful relations. Again, as noted in Chapter 3, mapping makes possible the practice of sovereign territorial jurisdiction. Maps can, of course, engage other jurisdictional relationships. The medieval *mappae mundi* offer one example. The Psalter *Mappa Mundi*, for example, shows Christ standing above the world, with outstretched arms; while Christ sits in judgment above the Hereford *Mappa Mundi* and the map revolves around Jerusalem, which is at the exact centre of the world. They were a projection of Christian truths onto a geographical framework. The maps, therefore, show a world structurally dependent on Christ and his earthly institution, the Church, reflecting the dominance of the Church in medieval life (Harvey 1996; Woodward 1991).

The Native Title Act 1993 (Cth), s 62 prescribes that, in order to register a claimant application for a determination of native title, certain information must be provided. The information required includes a map of the claim area and a detailed written description outlining the boundaries of the area covered by the claim area. As a result of this, the issue of mapping native title claim areas has become a complex one, requiring access to sophisticated geospatial data. The Geospatial Analysis and Mapping Branch of the National Native Title Tribunal produces geospatial technical guidelines for the preparation of maps to be used in claims. An application for native title requires a written boundary description. A written boundary description is one which 'defines an area of the earth's surface without ambiguity and having legal integrity'. It involves, a 'commencement point', proceeds 'in a clockwise direction', often uses 'co-ordinate points or pairs' and 'Australian Map Grid' references to two decimal places. A locality map should be included (National Native Title Tribunal (n.d.)). For a native title claim, therefore, the requirements of the Act may amount not only to a map and a written description of the claim area, but also pages and pages of detailed geographic co-ordinates: points of longitude and latitude in accordance with GDA94. These co-ordinates are required to pinpoint the exact boundaries of the claim area. For the claimants, however, the precision of Western mapping denies the complex nature of interrelations of law between families, clans and other groups. Western mapping practices reinforce the idea of the 'tribe' as a homogenous entity with clearly bounded borders and culture. Yet, for some claimants, the boundaries of their land may be incapable of such precise delineation in this way. For the Spinifex people, for example, there is no 'bright line' of territory or territorial jurisdiction.

While the paintings (maps) of the Spinifex people are a visual representation of their country, they were designed to be read by both indigenous and non-indigenous. The paintings not only tell us about the jurisprudence and law of the Spinifex people, they also indicate how the Spinifex people understand the Australian common law and its forms of representation. While the Spinifex maps were presented to the Federal Court as maps of country, authority and lawful relationships, in the final settlement approved by the court it was a Cartesian map, accompanied by co-ordinates of longitude and latitude, which denoted the successful claim area. There are a number of observations to be made about this. First, the meeting of laws was one determined by a common law jurisdiction and its forms of knowledge. In other words, the claimants were required to prove their interest according to the rules of the common law and the provisions of the Native Title Act 1993 (Cth). Second, the Spinifex case particularly reminds us about the way in which the maps of the common law are treated as representing a particular form of factual evidence. What this means is that for the common law side of the meeting of law, the representation of the land or country is not an acknowledgement of law but rather the marking of an empirical boundary. It is the technology and language of common law which is used to delimit the claim area. What is acknowledged in this technology is not so much another law and the people who live by it, but a physical mark. It is the significance of this representation of the meeting of laws as one of evidence, rather than the different modes of representation between the 'bright lines' of Cartesian maps and the paintings of the Spinifex people, to which we now turn.

In the final part of this section, we explore the significance of the way in which the common law characterises indigenous law in terms of fact. To do this, we turn to another common law technology of jurisdiction in order to see how the relationship between common law and indigenous law is named as 'native title'. Doctrinally, native title is the point of intersection between the common law and multiple indigenous jurisdictions. Here, we look at a technical piece of legislation – the Native Title Act 1993 (Cth) – and in particular s 223 which defines native title. Native title (as articulated in the decision of the High Court of Australia in *Mabo (No 2)*) describes the doctrine according to which the courts in Australia are willing to recognise at common law an interest in land which derives from the customary practices of the indigenous claimants. Section 223 of the Act defines native title for the purposes of that Act, providing basically that native title is a communal title to land and waters deriving from an ongoing connection with those lands and waters, the content of which is dependent on the particular customs of the particular indigenous claimant group. Section 223 appears to be a simple definitional provision. It is designed to enable the administration of the newly recognised indigenous rights and interests in a native title regime (how native title is claimed, and how it relates to other interests in land). However, s 223 is also a jurisdictional device. While avowedly neutral – it supposedly incorporates neither a moral or political stance on native title – it is not just technical. It engages particular forms of lawful conduct. Here we return to one of the technologies in Chapter 3, that of naming, in order to see how naming as an activity, and the relationships it engages, are a form of conduct.

In recognising native title, the decision in *Mabo (No 2)* created a relationship between two laws – those of the Meriam people and that of the common law of the Australian nation. The language of the Australian High Court itself recognised this to some extent, although it was clear from the beginning that this relationship was not necessarily from the perspective of that court one of legal equals. Nor was the High Court able to articulate with much clarity the nature of the relationship between these laws or the manner in which they engage. Famously, according to Brennan J, '[n]ative title has its origins in and is given its content by the traditional laws acknowledged by and the traditional customs observed by the indigenous inhabitants of a territory' (*Mabo (No 2)*, at 58; see also *Fejo v Northern Territory* (1998) 195 CLR 96, 128). In a later case, *The Wik Peoples*, Kirby J reminded us that even if native title were extinguished at common law, it might continue under indigenous law. The ceasing of recognition at common law he noted 'does not mean that, within in its own world, native title or any other incidents of the customary laws of Australia's indigenous peoples depends on the common law for its legitimacy or content' (*The Wik Peoples v Queensland* (1996) 187 CLR 1, 213). This, of course, left open the question of the form of those laws – 'law' or something lesser, to be thought of as 'custom'. The formulation of law as an intersection continues to be reiterated by courts, if somewhat formulaically.

If, according to the High Court, native title exists at the intersection of laws, then the question to be asked is where is the meeting place now located? One meeting place was established through the Native Title Act 1993 (Cth), s 223. While it is not, as such, an 'operational' section of the Act, after the enactment of the Act the High Court mandated that the location of the intersection between common law and indigenous law and custom must be located by reference to that Act (*Western Australia v Ward* (2002) 213 CLR 1, [16]). The court itself effectively relocated the meeting place of two laws to s 223. Thinking about the way in which s 223 works allows us to consider the ways in which a specific legal device creates legal relations. It also provides a way of drawing out the quality and the limits of legal engagement expressed within Australian common law.

The Native Title Act 1993 (Cth), s 223 was originally intended as a 'shell'. Its purpose was to provide a working definition of native title that would be broad enough to encapsulate a growing body of common law jurisprudence on native title. In jurisdictional terms, the meeting place remained within the common law itself, with s 223 designed as conduit between the common law and the Act. Every key phrase in s 223 has been subjected by the Federal Court to scrutiny and has resulted in a body of (not always entirely consistent) case law which presents significant barriers for claimants. The central concern of s 223 lies with the proof or evidence needed to establish 'rights and interests' under the Act. Key phrases include 'communal, group or individual', 'rights and interests . . . in relation to land and waters', 'traditional laws acknowledged', 'traditional customs observed' and 'connection'.

Over the last decade, the continual tightening of the interpretation of these words in the Native Title Act 1993 (Cth), s 223 by the Federal Court of Australia has crafted a 'fragmented' or highly individuated view of indigenous law through native title (McHugh 2011). One example of the way in which 'rights and interests' in s 223 are interpreted is the problem of including what might be termed a claim for the 'right to speak for country' within the rights recognisable in that section. For indigenous Australians, a right to speak for country encompasses the rights and responsibilities of the traditional owners of the land to speak about the care of country and of their inherent rights to land and waters. In *The Lardil Peoples*, for example, the claim included the right to speak for country with respect to an area offshore. Olney J in that case noted that: 'to state the right as "a right to speak for Country" lacks the precision required by the Act. In fact it is the expression of a concept which embraces a 'bundle of rights' varying in number and kind, which may or may not be capable of full or accurate expression as rights to control what others may or may not do with the land and waters' (*Lardil Peoples v Queensland* [2004] FCA 298, [71]). Rather than a recognition of a right of custodianship for country, or of a right to participate in decision-making with respect to the area, Olney J transformed a right to speak for country to a question of right to access or right to control access to the claimed area. The judgment further fragmented or individuated the reasons for which access would be allowed, most of which boiled down to hunting and fishing (for subsistence) and ceremonial purposes (at [7]). Such claims, however, continue to be made by claimants, although more generally phrased now as a 'right to protect'. In *Sampi*, for example, the right claimed was 'the right to care for, maintain and protect the sea, including its places of spiritual or cultural importance'. The trial judge indicated that: 'I do not consider the claimed right to "care for, maintain and protect the land . . ." defines with any useful precision the nature of the entitlement which it confers or the activities which it will authorise' (*Sampi v Western Australia* (2005) FCA 777, [1073] per French J). Similarly, in *Neowarra*, Sundberg J included in the determination of native title a right to visit places and protect them from physical harm. He stated that:

The evidence is that maintaining places of importance involves low impact activities such as visiting, checking for damage, smoking, speaking to the Wanjina [spirit ancestor] and repainting. Activities of this type are not inconsistent with a pastoralist's right to graze stock. In the event of a clash of activities at or near a particular site, the pastoralist's right will prevail. Protection is directed to the prevention of damage to sites. . . . This might involve Aboriginal presence when a busload of tourists visits a painting location, to ensure that the site is not damaged.

> (*Neowarra v Western Australia* [2003] FCA 1402, [484])

In a conventional sense the Native Title Act 1993 (Cth), s 223 is a definitional section. It defines the concept of 'native title' for the purposes of the Act. Hence, s 223 was designed to negotiate the relationship between statute and the common law, not the common law and indigenous jurisdictions (law). If s 223 is simply a definitional section, then its role is neutral. However, the section has been used to establish relations between jurisdictions as predominantly evidential. In other words, the relations between s 223 and indigenous jurisdictions is presented and represented in terms of a concern with evidence and proof. Such a relationship is, in a sense, sceptical. Section 223, as a jurisdictional device, addresses itself, repeatedly, as to whether there is another law – as to whether traditional laws and customs exist. The meeting of law is created through the procedures of inquiry and contest established through native title regulation. The jurisdictional relationship, therefore, between the common law jurisdiction and indigenous jurisdictions can be characterised as one in which the relationship remained one of proof and evidence. The result is that a simple definitional/proof section has been transformed to a jurisdictional 'limitation point'.

As a definitional provision the Native Title Act 1993 (Cth), s 223 need not have taken on the central position in native title doctrine that it has. The relocation of the meeting point of laws to s 223, however, has been transformative in a number of ways. First, s 223 has taken on what might be described as an active jurisdictional role. Rather than being definitional, it has become, in a sense, operative, or at least has become treated as such. However, if s 223 has an evidential character, it also has taken on an active expression of a lawful relation. To emphasise the active quality of native title is to point to the procedures of law in terms of the quality of conduct or action. When Bentham and English analytical jurisprudents linked adjective law, including evidence and procedure, with the administration of justice, they did so by way of contrast with substantive law (Bentham 1843: 13). Here we emphasise the dynamic account of legal activity. Viewed in this way s 223 joins a jurisdictional account of how we conduct ourselves through law. It becomes a part of the protocols of the engagement of law.

By re-locating the meeting point of laws in statute, and as a result of the High Court's insistence that the intersection or meeting place is the Native Title Act 1993 (Cth), s 223, that section has become a jurisdictional technology or device capable of authorising, locating, changing, and figuring legal relations. One obvious example of a jurisdictional device from the history of the common law is the writ of prohibition. This was a writ used by the common law to take jurisdiction from other jurisdictions. The example of the writ of prohibition, however, pre-supposes that the purpose of such a device is to order relations between acknowledged and existing laws – to configure a meeting point. Historically, that meeting point might have been, for example, between common law and ecclesiastical law. It is easier to see something like this writ functioning as a technology or device of jurisdiction, and actively crafting legal relations, because we recognised both jurisdictions. It is a different matter, however, to see something like s 223 as a jurisdictional device when one of the laws remains unacknowledged.

The Native Title Act 1993 (Cth), s 223 names a relationship of two laws. It also names the forms of conduct appropriate to such a meeting of laws. Holding such accounts of conduct to jurisdictional practice allows for a clear consideration of the quality of lawful relations expressed through the Australian common law tradition. It also points to the extremely restricted forms of engagement that the Australian common law envisages. It shows in an appallingly stark manner the ways in which those who live by the forms of Australian common law and jurisprudence are prepared to meet those who live by indigenous laws and jurisprudence.

Concluding comments

In this chapter we have investigated a number of ways in which forms of jurisdictional practice have shaped and created relations between laws. Our concern here has been with the different forms of articulation and expression of lawful relations through the operation of the technologies and practices of common law jurisdiction. We have tracked some of the ways in which such meeting places have been established and, by implication, the sorts of meeting place that might be imagined.

As in Chapter 5, we have divided our concern with jurisdictional meeting place of laws between the jurisdictions of civility and conscience. In this chapter, we have presented our analysis of the meeting place of laws predominantly in terms of the authority of civil jurisdiction. As understood by the common law this meeting place has been concerned with the status of the sovereignty of common law and a consideration of indigenous and non-indigenous relations in terms of governance and welfare. In this chapter, more so than the others, there are different paths available through which to analyse the practices of jurisdiction. Many of the critical comments we have made about the form of territorial jurisdiction have also been expressed in forms of social and cultural theory concerned with questions of identity and subjectivity, and with questions of political domination and oppression. In the form of analysis presented here, many of these concerns could be expressed from within a jurisdiction of conscience. They address the formation of the legal subject and the conditions of freedom. In a jurisdiction of conscience, what is offered is a politics of recognition that is attuned to questions of the acknowledgement of the common humanity and shared political concerns of indigenous and non-indigenous peoples. In contemporary debates about the meeting place of laws, we often use languages of value that can carry meaning as a matter both of civility and conscience. So terms like dignity, rights, autonomy and self-determination are often used to engage the two forms of jurisdictional authority. However, our analysis offers reasons why such accounts of dignity and rights should be treated with care. It is the practices of jurisdiction that provide the craft and form of life of lawful relations that are brought to the meeting place of laws.

The contemporary mixing of jurisdictions and the comparative lack of institutional shaping of jurisdictions of conscience mean that most institutional understanding of law tends to be conducted through the jurisdiction of civil authority. As our analysis has suggested, where critical and transformative engagements of law rest on jurisdictions of conscience, it is difficult to gain purchase on the jurisdictional forms that might be appropriate to the task. This concern becomes pivotal when we begin to consider how much life can or should be engaged through the common law. The formulation of relations of civil authority requires only a thin account of the meeting place of laws. The formulations of the civil jurisdiction leave much for an engagement 'beyond' law. The jurisdictions of conscience require more fully elaborated forms of conduct. Raimond Gaita, for example, has argued that Brennan J's judgment in *Mabo (No 2)* not only engaged with the technical ordering of a meeting of laws but also with the quality of the meeting. For Brennan, according to Gaita, what is at issue is the acknowledgement of common humanity and of the full humanity of indigenous people. Without this, Gaita argues, there can be no question of a just meeting of laws – and no meeting place worthy of its name (Gaita 1999: 77–85).

There is a sense in which our chapter is subject to the same criticisms as we have made of the common law. The meeting of laws is not entered into with sufficient seriousness. A meeting of laws and a meeting place requires at least two laws. One law must witness and engage another. In this sense, even an account of lawful relations which is limited to an exploration of forms of common law jurisdiction needs to be witnessed by the laws it meets. The refusal of the form of the maps of the Spinifex people in the *Spinifex* claim, and the consequent presentation of law by the courts, would be an example of a refusal of the witnessing of law. The law of the Spinifex people was treated only as evidence of custom.

Kombumerri/Munaljarlai jurisprudent Christine Black makes two points in relation to the witness and meeting of laws (Black 2011a). The first is that a proper meeting of laws involves a witnessing of lawful behaviour (one's own and that of another). Such witnessing would require that those who follow the common law know something of the laws with which they wish to engage. The common law must be able to see its law as witnessed through indigenous laws and jurisprudence (Black 2011b: 358). The second point to be addressed is a concern with the quality of the law through which we meet. In this chapter, we have outlined some of the technologies of jurisdiction with which the common law creates the places in which we dwell, and the mode and manner with which it addresses other laws. The common law technologies provide a limited repertoire of engagements, delimited for the most part by the concerns of a civil jurisdiction. Christine Black points out that such jurisprudential concerns – roughly those of responsibilities and rights – form only one part of 'a continuous feeling for the web of interconnected relationships that pattern humans into their environment' (Black 2011a: 12). From within her own *talngai-gawarima* jurisprudence, Black points to the ways in which indigenous jurisprudences can be shaped in terms of three concentric circles. The outermost circle is that of *cosmology*, the story (or theory) of 'how people are patterned into the land'. The second circle is *the law of relationship*. It encompasses the sense of lawfulness that arises from the land. The pattern of this relationship is 'dyadic' or twofold. Relationships are structured or patterned as complementary, rather than as oppositional relations. Finally, then, the inner circle relates to the *responsibilities and rights* that arise when relations to the land are taken up. The voice of authority is 'born out of experience and actualisation of law' (Black 2011a: 15–16). Viewed in this way, the responsibilities of an indigenous law encompass far more than the common law can admit in its limited responsibility for law. Likewise, what is brought to a meeting place of law is a series of responsibilities and rights with which common law jurisprudence has to be brought into relation (in order to sustain a relation to the law of the land).

In the more prudential analysis offered here, it is the limited responsibility (or structured irresponsibility) of the civil jurisdiction that has dominated the common law understanding of the meeting places of law (Veitch 2007: ch 3). For many critics, the common law tradition has shown itself incapable of responding adequately to the responsibility of engaging meaningfully or justly in a meeting of laws. This might be understood in terms of the limits of the civil form of engagement with justice that Brennen J permitted himself in *Mabo (No 2)*. His concern with maintaining the integrity of the common law, and his acceptance that sovereign acts of states such as the acquisition of colonies are non-justiciable, were failures of responsibility. While the Native Title Act 1993 (Cth) deflects this concern with the experience of law by establishing an administrative domain, it does so by effacing the concern with the conduct of the meeting of laws. The resources of conduct provided through contemporary native title regulation provide limited scope through which to engage lawful relations.

In this chapter, we have investigated a number of ways in which native title as a jurisdictional device creates forms of lawful relation. It is clear that many native title determinations have created relations that acknowledge very little indigenous law and jurisprudence. Within the common law tradition, the office of judge and jurist has had responsibility for the naming, ordering and locating of legal relations. The practices that shape the jurisdictional form of native title are part of a long tradition of engagement of customary or common laws. Part of an ethic of responsibility for the form of law is, no doubt, to be framed in terms of finding the appropriate internal qualities of law to meet the external realities it addresses. This, it might be imagined, could require acknowledgement that the jurisdictional practices of native title are a part of the creation of meeting places of law; or, for example, that the jurisdictional practices of the common law operate in ways that offer a wholly inadequate meeting place of laws.

Notes

1 The term '*tjukrrpa*' encompasses both spiritual and other aspects, including notions of law, ownership, etc (see Cane 2002: 16). For a more detailed consideration, see Dorsett 2007: 137–159.
2 Maralinga tests – 54,000 km2 consent determination 2000, see *Anderson v Western Australia* [2000] FCA 1717.

References

Bentham, J. (1843) *Principles of Judicial Procedure*, in Bowring, J. (ed), *The Works of Jeremy Bentham*, Edinburgh: William Tait.

Black, C.F. (2011a) *The Land is the Source of the Law*, London: Routledge.

Black, C.F (2011b) 'Maturing Australia Through Australian Aboriginal Narrative Law', *The South Atlantic Quarterly* 110: 347–362.

Cane, S. (2002) *Pila Nguru: The Spinifex People*, Fremantle: Fremantle Arts Centre Press.

Dorsett, S. and McVeigh, S. (2005) 'Jurisprudence. Jurisdiction and Authority in *Yorta Yorta*', *Northern Ireland Legal Quarterly* 59: 1–20.

Dorsett, S. (2007) 'Mapping Territory', in McVeigh, S. (ed), *On the Jurisprudence of Jurisdiction*, London: Routledge-Cavendish.

Gaita, R. (1999) *A Common Humanity*, Melbourne: Text Publishing.

Harvey, P.D.A. (1996) *Mappae Mundi: The Hereford World Map*, Toronto: University of Toronto Press.

McHugh, P.G. (2011) *Aboriginal Title: The Modern Jurisprudence of Tribal Land Rights*, Oxford: Oxford University Press.

National Native Title Tribunal (n.d.) *Guidelines for Written Boundary Descriptions Associated with Native Title Applications and Indigenous Land Use Agreements*, <http://www.nntt.gov.au/Publications-And-Research/Maps-and-Spatial-Reports/Documents/Guidelines_for_written_boundary_descriptions.pdf> (accessed 23 November 2011).

Rush, P. (1997a) 'Deathbound Doctrine: Scenes of Murder and Its Inheritance', *Studies in Law, Politics and Society* 16: 69–97.

Rush, P. (1997b) 'An Altered Jurisdiction: Corporeal Traces of Law', *Griffith Law Review* 6: 144–168.

Veitch, S. (2007) *Law and Irresponsibility: On the Legitimation of Human Suffering*, London: Routledge.

Woodward, D. (1991) 'Maps and the Rationalization of Geographic Space', in Levenson, J. (ed), *Circa 1492: Art in the Age of Exploration*, New Haven, CT and National Gallery of Art, Washington, DC: Yale University Press.

Chapter 7

Jurisdiction, events and the international

The making and re-making of the international domain has been one of the most striking political and economic events since 1945. We hear much about 'globalisation' and the redundancy of the old (European) political order of sovereign states. However, we continue to struggle to give juridical shape and meaning to the ways in which the legal orders, regimes, modes of government and administration are created and sustained as international, transnational and global activities. In our studies in Chapters 5 and 6, we align jurisdiction with persons and place; here, we turn attention to forms of jurisdiction ordered around events or activities. We address the jurisdiction of events in terms of the ways in which jurisdictional practices shape the representation of the community of international law.

As with other chapters in this book, we focus on the crafting of lawful relations rather than on forms of political theology, social theory or cultural explanation. We treat events and activities as taking on meaning through jurisdictional practices. This gives us a point of ordering for a consideration of the way in which events or activities are engaged through forms of jurisdictional practice. The first part of this chapter concentrates on the jurisdictional form of the meeting of sovereign territorial states and the relation of the meeting to forms of jurisdictional authority. It addresses the rival forms of jurisdiction and rival representations of European relations of religion and empire that have characterised much of international activity. The second part addresses the event or activity of decolonisation. We set this concern in relation to decolonisation post-1939–1945 and the claim to permanent sovereignty over natural resources. The third part attends to the forms of jurisdiction and community brought into relation in response to a particular event. Here we focus our attention on the Eichmann trial, which was one response to the genocide of European Jewry by the Nazi regime. The trial of Adolf

Eichmann in Israel in 1961 has, for many, become emblematic of the jurisdictional shape of the international domain. It allows us to see how an event – genocide – can create and represent a jurisdiction of conscience. In the final part of this chapter, we briefly examine the forms of community and repertoires of conscience through which critical jurists have addressed jurisdictions of international law.

In considering how a jurisdiction can be shaped around an event, we are drawing on arguments from earlier chapters. For example, in Chapter 3, we considered the ways in which we represent authority. In that chapter, we also see one example of how an event can shape a jurisdiction. There we see the ways in which a jurisdiction (the *lex mercatoria*) is shaped around the event of the fair. In Chapter 4, we considered the technologies which bring events into relation with law – in particular, the technologies of representation.

Jurisdiction and forms of the international

Whilst today there is little serious discussion about the existence of an international domain and the status of international law as international law, there is still a considerable dispute about its authority, modes of operation and address. It is to be expected that sovereign territorial states feature in the representations of the international. Here, however, we pluralise the representation of the international in three ways. First, we point to the plurality of international orders; second, we draw out the diversity of jurisdictional thought in international law; and, third, we address the international order represented by the United Nations.

Framed in terms of jurisdictional arrangements, we can begin by noting the plurality of jurisdictional forms of the international. International law, or the law between and amongst nations, need not be restricted to the contemporary expansion and development of European public international law or of private international law. While accounts of international law and international relations are typically presented from this viewpoint, there have been significant rival international orders. The jurist Onuma (Onuma 2000) points to forms of Islam and Chinese international law that existed through to the end of the 19th century. To this can be added the many forms of international law and relations created and practised by indigenous peoples. Indigenous orderings of international relations predate the generalisation of European public international law. The Western legal traditions have only recently begun to engage with these international laws (Glenn 2010).

If we turn our attention to contemporary forms of international law, the international domain is marked by a huge variety of jurisdictional arrangements, instruments and devices. At the risk of caricature, since the 17th century, jurists have tended to present the international according to two rival accounts – one giving shape to the international domain in terms of the free meeting of sovereign territorial nation states, the other shaping the international domain around forms of cosmopolitan order that treat the international domain as having an independent existence. In its stronger versions, these accounts treat international law as a form of general law of the world and, in some aspects at least, a universal law. The contemporary international legal order lives with both of these ways of thinking about international law (Hunter 2001, 2010).

The formulation of international law as a manifestation of the sovereign will of the state, albeit one shaped by custom, justice and the need for peace and order, still lies at the centre of international law thinking (if not practice). The treaties, instruments, covenants and statutes, and its modes of government and adjudication of the international domain, are shaped as if they were the negotiated outcome of sovereign acts. This view of international law has a long history. It is consonant with a tradition of the international that developed in the 16th century in Europe and a series of treaties now known as the Treaty of Westphalia (1648), briefly discussed in Chapter 2. These treaties, viewed retrospectively and selectively, have been taken as marking the origin of European public international law. On the one hand, the treaties marked a decisive break with the authority of the Holy Roman Empire and the (Roman) Catholic Church over temporal matters in the sovereign kingdoms of Europe. The law of sovereign nation states was to be framed as a matter of temporal authority. On the other hand, the treaties established the outlines of a system of European territorial states between which peaceful relations should be maintained and an 'open' space outside of Europe, free for appropriation. The formulation of this understanding of the international domain was very much the work of jurists and theologians working from the 15th to the end of the 19th century (Hobbes 1968; Grotius 2005; Pufendorf 2009). These accounts of the international domain not only set in place the understanding of the international as the meeting of nations, they also provided the repertoires and characters (conceptual *personae*) who inhabit this domain. On the positive side, these writings provided ways of thinking about the international domain as a site of diplomacy, free exchange and competitive engagement. On the negative side, they also identified those 'uncivilised' people who were not fit for the international domain and those, like pirates, who were the enemies of mankind (Pagden 1998; Anghie 2005).

In the early part of the last century, the judicial understanding of the international domain was largely organised around sovereign territorial states. The *SS Lotus Case* (1927) of the Permanent Court of International Justice is often cited for its characterisation of international law in terms of the government of relations between independent sovereign states. Such law was viewed by the court in terms of agreements entered into by states as a matter of their own free will (*SS Lotus (Fr v Turk)*, 1927 PCIJ (Ser A) No 10). States have an independent legal personality capable of acting and being acted upon at the level of international relations. The international domain has also been peopled with a range of international organisations since 1927, but this understanding of international law stills forms an important part of contemporary debates about the character of the international domain.

Reflecting the continuing importance of state sovereignty, we might note the jurisdiction of the main international adjudicatory body, the International Court of Justice. States must consent to appear before that court in contentious matters. Where a state does not consent, the court cannot hear the matter (*Treatment in Hungary of Aircraft and Crew of the United States of America (United States of America v Hungary) (United States of America v USSR)* 1954 ICJ Rep 103). While states can lodge declarations recognizing the compulsory jurisdiction of the court under the Statute of the International Court of Justice, Art 36(2), only 66 nations have lodged such declarations, and these countries do not include the United States, Russia or China. The International Court of Justice also has an advisory jurisdiction which can be accessed by non-sovereign international organisations. This is non-binding, although parties can stipulate that the judgment is to have binding effect. The voluntary character of the International Court of Justice leaves sovereign authority at the level of the sovereign territorial state. We should note, however, that there are many institutional arrangements of the international domain that are far from voluntary. Think, for example, of the authority and jurisdiction of the World Bank.

Alongside this state-centred account of the international domain there have also been a number of rival accounts of the international. Historically, the most important of these has been the presence, revival and elaboration of forms of universal jurisdiction. The formulation of universal arrangements has a long history. For jurisprudents there are models of cosmopolitan citizenship from Roman jurisprudence that imagine forms of law appropriate to the obligations of a citizen of the world (Shapcott 2010). The traditions of Catholic thought, as we will see, have provided us with distinct forms of spiritual and temporal jurisdiction. In medieval Europe, the universal spiritual jurisdiction of the Pope was matched by the universal temporal jurisdiction of the Holy Roman Emperor. These concerns still give shape to contemporary understanding and aspirations of international jurisdictions. Internationalists need jurisdictional forms to craft the lawful relations of the international domain.

The emergence of international institutions in the 20th century has been shaped by both versions of international jurisdiction. From the end of the First World War, an increasing number of international organisations were brought into existence, starting with the formation of the League of Nations (1919) and the Permanent Court of International Justice (1921), and taking shape round the United Nations (1948) and the covenants on civil and political rights and on economic, social and cultural rights (1966).

For the purposes of this chapter, one jurisdiction is presented clearly in the opening Article of the Charter of the United Nations of 1945. It sets out its purposes in Art 1 as follows:

1. To maintain international peace and security, to take effective collective measures for the prevention and removal of threats to the peace, and for the suppression of acts of aggression or other breaches of the peace, and to bring about by peaceful means, and in conformity with the principles of justice and international law, adjustment or settlement of international disputes or situations which might lead to a breach of the peace;

2. To develop friendly relations among nations based on respect for the principle of equal rights and self-determination of peoples, and to take other appropriate measures to strengthen universal peace;

3. To achieve international co-operation in solving international problems of an economic, social, cultural, or humanitarian character, and in promoting and encouraging respect for human rights and for fundamental freedoms for all without distinction as to race, sex, language, or religion; and

4. To be a center for harmonizing the actions of nations in the attainment of these common ends.

While the Charter of the United Nations does not embody the international, it has increasingly become the emblematic representation around which institutional forms of the international domain are organised. The United Nations, then, was to be concerned with the creation and administration of an international domain by 'taking measures', 'solving international problems' and 'encouraging respect'. All this was to be achieved through the United Nations acting as a 'center for harmonizing'. This image of the United Nations as a diplomatic space of harmonisation prevailed until the turn of this century. Here, we point to the way in which the image of the United Nations as a site of harmonisation and diplomacy is a jurisdictional exercise of authority.

For the most part, the institutional documents of the United Nations do not concern themselves with matters of jurisdiction. In fact, the United Nations, particularly through the Security Council, determines its own jurisdiction (*Reparations for Injuries Suffered in the Service of the United Nations (Advisory Opinion)* [I 949] ICJ Rep 174). Anne Orford has recently argued that these jurisdictional arrangements in many ways return to earlier jurisdictional forms practised by the (Roman) Catholic Church and the Holy Roman Empire. The jurisdictions of the Catholic Church and the Holy Roman Empire were universal and not territorial. The Pope exercised jurisdiction over the spiritual realm, and the Holy Roman Emperor over the temporal realm. The jurisdiction of the Holy Roman Emperor was universal and not limited by territory. The Emperor had dominion over the world as a whole. As Orford points out, this is a jurisdiction exercised as of right and was treated by apologists as being of a different order to the types of jurisdictions exercised by sovereigns such as the King of France (Orford 2011: 148–150).

In modern terms, the international executive of the United Nations, for example the Security Council, acts in the name of the universal, particularly in the domains of fact-finding and peacekeeping, It also establishes a jurisdiction without territory. This form of international ordering, particularly when considered in the light of the development of international organisations, such as those of finance and trade (the World Bank, the International Monetary Fund and the World Trade Organisation), shows an international sphere has established forms of jurisdictional existence independent of the direct authority of sovereign territorial states. Orford's account reminds us that the international domain was not, and is not, peopled solely by territorial sovereigns. Whether or not contemporary forms of jurisdiction establish a new Empire is, of course, open to dispute. We simply point out that, as elsewhere, the technologies of jurisdiction have survived over long periods. No doubt, the lawful relations established by such jurisdictional arrangements have changed.

Rival jurisdictions: permanent sovereignty over natural resources

One way we have framed jurisdictional relationships has been through the meeting of laws. This was considered, for example, in Chapter 6 in the context of the meeting of indigenous and non-indigenous jurisdictions. In this section, we follow this meeting into the international through what we called, in Chapter 5, a jurisdiction of civility. Here, the meeting of sovereign territorial states is represented as a meeting of equals. The Charter of the United Nations suggests that one purpose of the United Nations is the promotion of amity and the diminution of emnity between states. The utopian promise of the Charter is that these relations will be framed as an engagement between equals in the name of the universal values expressed in the Charter and in declarations of the United Nations. This is often represented as a narrative of development and of nations becoming progressively more equal. Here, however, we point to the ways in which the complex relations of jurisdiction between the national and the international domain and between international institutions themselves represent a hierarchy of power and authority.

We offer a brief example here that belongs to the age of de-colonisation and the claims by the newly independent states to control their natural resources (McVeigh and Pahuja 2009). The post-1945 independence movements were in many ways a triumph against empire (Orford 2011). The founding of the United Nations provided a parallel assertion of the foundation of a new international order that is no longer described as a European international law. However, as many third world scholars have noted, the outcomes have rarely turned out this way (Rajagopal 2003; Chatterjee 1993). If we look, for example, at the claims made for a right to assert or retain permanent sovereignty over natural resources (PSNR), we can see that the formal equality of sovereign states in reality left little room for substantive claims of sovereignty. The claim for permanent control of natural resources is a claim of the right to control the exploitation of natural resources. On gaining independence in the post-war period many new states attempted to 'nationalise' natural resources, such as oil and minerals, and 'return' them to the control of nation and the state. The rights to exploit these resources had been granted to, and fought for by, international companies as part of 19th- and early 20th-century colonisation. Contemporary equivalents might be found in Iraq and the re-allocation of oil licences. The assertion of this claim of sovereignty by the new states was met in a number of ways. The first was that disputes should be heard in the domain of international law, and the second was that remedies should be given in terms of compensation. The reasons offered for this formulation might be summarised in terms of the maintenance of property and the insistence that contracts must be honoured (*pacta sunt servanda*). While many contested the quality of compensation and the precise formulation of the maintenance of international contracts (Hossain 1984), what is harder to keep visible is that that such assertions are assertions of a rival jurisdiction.

While the image of the international is one of the meeting of equal states, the presumed existence of an international law means that the newly decolonised nations joined an international domain that already constrained what could be asserted by way of sovereignty (Pahuja 2011b). The new states arrived at the meeting place in the spirit of speaking and acting in their own names (asserting their own jurisdiction) but what happened was that joining the international domain meant speaking, and being spoken to, through the form of an existing international jurisdiction. The insistence by international companies that mining and mineral concessions be protected as property rights capable of compensation might be viewed itself as a masked assertion of a kind of non-state sovereignty (Pahuja 2011b). However, if we follow the jurisdictional arrangement of disputes over PSNR a clearer picture of rival claims emerges. The disputes over PSNR were not met in the international domain as claims of sovereign self-determination but rather were reframed as ones that involved the resolution of property rights and, indirectly, as matters of the maintenance of trust and confidence in the international financial order. If new states simply refused to offer compensation for the nationalisation of resources, it was argued, then the conditions for international finance and investment would fail. (There are some clear parallels in the current European debt crisis.) Framed in this way, the question of PSNR became a matter of financial governance and a concern of the newly formed World Bank established under the Bretton-Woods agreements (Pahuja 2011b). This, we argue, is best understood as an exercise of the jurisdiction of the World Bank – an exercise of jurisdiction, it might be added, that is not subject to accountability (McVeigh and Pahuja 2009). We frame these arguments here in terms of rival jurisdictions because the power or authority to decide, to determine the conditions of dispute, is precisely what is being contested.

In recent work, Sundhya Pahuja (2011a) has set the representation of the jurisdictions of international institutions in two broader frames of reference. The first of these is the political form of development, and the second is the ambivalence of the claims and promise of universal human rights. On the question of development, Pahuja points out that the claim of PSNR started out first and foremost as a political claim about the conditions of meeting as a community of states in the international domain. However, it continues as an argument about securing the necessary means for the development of what was the third world (political) and is now framed in terms of the global south (Pahuja 2011b). The development story, both critical and uncritical, is not usually one considered in terms of jurisdiction. In its broad form it is marked by a concern with ensuring the development of the economic, cultural and political resources of poorer nations. These nations by-and-large were once colonised by European powers and are now governed in relation to the management of debt and the development of capabilities for self-government. Critics of development projects have pointed out the ways in which much of the poverty of poorer nations is held in place by an international legal order that facilitates the transmission of resources from the poor to the rich (Orford 2001; Pogge 2005). The political forms and narratives of progress and development are complex and much of it can be analysed without reference to jurisdiction. However, paying attention to jurisdiction allows us to analyse the forms and practices of authority that shape international political economy and international law. This is important because it allows us to address the forms of authority and community established in the international domain without succumbing either to the representation of the international as being the site of the realisation of human rights or as being a domain only of domination and exploitation.

Universal jurisdiction – the event of the Eichmann trial

In order to examine the ways in which a supra-national jurisdiction is developed out of certain events or activities, we turn here to the trial of Adolf Eichmann, before the District Court in Jerusalem, for crimes committed against Jews during the Second World War. In 1960, the government of Israel seized Adolf Eichmann in Argentina and took him to Israel for trial. Eichmann was in charge of section IV B4 of the Gestapo, which was charged with Jewish affairs and emigration. In this capacity he oversaw, and was responsible for, the administrative details and management of the final destruction of the Jewish people of Nazi-occupied Europe. The trial of the German Eichmann is considered by many to be the first to take up a jurisdiction, to take responsibility, and to exercise authority, in the matter of 'crimes against humanity'. Much of the judgment is concerned with whether the state of Israel could take jurisdiction. By concentrating on a jurisdictional analysis, this example shows the difficulties of producing a juridical sphere apart from the territorial nation state. The Eichmann trial was one of the first attempts by a national court to exercise jurisdiction over a human rights violation conducted outside its borders, by someone not a citizen of that country.

As we noted in Chapter 1, the trial was for acts committed outside the bounds of the state, against a person who was not an Israeli citizen, by a person who acted in the course of duty on behalf of a foreign country, and for acts committed before Israel existed (*Government of Israel v Adolph Eichmann* 36 IRL 5, [8], Dist Court Jerusalem, affd 36 ILR 277, reprinted in (1962) 56 *Am J Int'l L* 805). Eichmann was charged under a specific statute, the Nazis and Nazi Collaborators (Punishment) Law 1950. That Act asserted jurisdiction over Nazi suspects. However, while Eichmann was charged under this statute, as the judgment makes clear in the end the court did not see this as the only, or perhaps sufficient, basis for jurisdiction. The court found that the statute 'conforme[d] to the best traditions of the law of nations' (at [11]). For the court, Israel's jurisdiction or, as the court put it, its 'right to punish' was based on the 'universal character of the crimes in question and their specific character as being designed to exterminate the Jewish people' (at [11]). In the Eichmann trial, the authority to try is explicitly derived from universal norms of customary international law. The court asserted the power or right to punish because 'the crimes . . . afflicted the whole of mankind and shocked the conscience of nations [and] are grave offences against the law of nations itself . . . The authority and jurisdiction to try crimes under international law are *universal*' (at [12]).

The court in the Eichmann trial is forced to rely on universal jurisdiction, and in particular on norms of customary international law, for two reasons. First, despite the clear assertion of jurisdiction over Nazi suspects in the Nazis and Nazi Collaborators (Punishment) Law 1950, it was far from clear that a national court could found its jurisdiction over a suspect who was not a citizen, for crimes committed before the existence of that nation state, against those who were not yet citizens themselves (Mann 2010: 493).[1] Nor could they rely on the most obvious other mechanism, the Genocide Convention. While that convention allowed a 'competent tribunal' (such as the Jerusaleum court) to assert jurisdiction over persons charged with genocide, that jurisdiction was bound to the territory of the nation state. Territorial jurisdiction was a pre-condition. The court itself recognised this, referring to 'territorial jurisdiction as a compulsory minimum' (at [19]). How then to shape a juridical sphere that was not reliant on territorial sovereignty and the nation state? And in doing so, what is to be bound to law if not territory? Customary international law and universal jurisdiction could not only provide this sphere, but remove the need for an international tribunal – any court could assert jurisdiction.

In establishing its jurisdiction, the court looks to the history of 'universal authority', drawing on jurists such as Grotius, Blackstone and Vattel. What the court found there is a long-standing 'right to punish' for the crime of piracy as a crime against the whole of humanity (*hostis humani generis*) which, drawing on this broadly, imposed a 'moral duty [on] every sovereign state (of the "kings and any who have rights equal to the rights of kings") to enforce the natural right to punish, possessed by the victims of the crime whoever they may be, against criminals whose acts have "violated in extreme form the law of nature or the law of nations"' (at [14]). After the Second World War, and based on principles adopted by the United Nations War Crimes Commission, a number of modern jurists articulated a 'general doctrine' of universality of jurisdiction under which independent states could punish not just pirates, but war criminals (for example, Cowles 1945). Through its examination of the right to punish, the court creates what Robert Cover might term a natural law of jurisdiction – one where the crime is so terrible that we must have a hearing and a punishment (Cover 1993).

What event is represented in the jurisdictional arrangements of the Eichmann trial? Here, the event might not only be considered as that of a trial or even a show trial, but also that of the mass extermination of Jews during the holocaust. Hannah Arendt famously argued that the wrong in the Eichmann trial was so new and so particular that it required and created a new jurisdiction (Arendt 2006: 253ff). For Arendt, what binds the event of the holocaust to law is its articulation within a jurisdiction of universal conscience. This helps us understand the way in which the exercise of a universal jurisdiction draws on and develops a jurisdiction of conscience. However, in our analysis what is bound and what is represented remain a matter of jurisdictional dispute. For us, the conscience of common humanity and the 'moral duty' of the sovereign remain concerns of rival jurisdictions.

Critics of international jurisdiction

More so perhaps than in other areas of law, international law engages directly with the work of jurists. The work of scholars, such as Lauterpacht or Crawford, continues to be a formal source of law under the Statute of International Court of Justice, Art 38(1)(d). This chapter closes with a brief consideration of the jurisdiction of the critics of international law and of the responsibilities associated with the forms of jurisdictional analysis of the events and activities presented in this chapter.

We turn briefly to two critical approaches to the international domain that draw out the responsibilities of the office of the critic. The first approach is drawn from a group of jurists and scholars who are associated with Third World Approaches to International Law (TWAIL), and the second addresses the forms of responsibility associated with acknowledging humanity in the context of crimes against humanity. TWAIL writings address the representation of the political, cultural and economic relations that structure international scholarship and the international domain. In so doing, they point to the dangers of representing the promise of international law as an emancipatory and universal order (Eslava and Pahuja 2011). As we saw in the first part of this chapter, in many ways international projects are yet to come to terms with imperial and colonial inheritances. Critics like Chimni and Rajagopal have pointed out that claims to universality expressed in the form of human rights frequently turn out to be generalisations of the specific interests and understandings of the people who created the human rights. So the rights of the Universal Declaration of Human Rights turn out to be shaped by the interests and desires of the declarers. These, for the most part, are the bearers of first world concerns. One consequence of this is that international projects fail to address the sources of injustice in the international domain (Rajagopal 2003; Chimni 2006).

The point that TWAIL scholars are making here is not that all invocations of universal values are wrong. Rather, they warn against authorising lawful relations by asserting universal values. In particular they point to the need to attend to the authority and conduct of lawful relations of the particular jurisdictions that express such universal values (de Sousa Santos and Rodriguez-Garavito 2005). The work of TWAIL jurists and scholars can be understood as the investigation of the jurisdictional and juridical forms appropriate to establishing the lawful relations of the global south. Some forms of lawful relations will address rights and responsibilities that are universal in character (for example responsibilities that are taken up as a matter of common humanity or for the care of the earth). The issue for TWAIL is how to address such concerns from a particular place (Black *et al* 2007, Minson 2009).

The final point of this chapter is addressed to the community engaged through the emergence of international jurisdiction over crimes against humanity such as genocide. If the office of the jurist cares for the legal form of such engagement, how might this be characterised in terms of jurisdiction and its community? In Chapter 2 we begin an answer to this kind of question by suggesting that part of a critical approach to law is to provide forms of jurisdiction adequate to the experience of those who engage with jurisdiction. Here, we have broadened our understanding of the office of the critic by considering whether a jurisdiction was adequate to those who suffered the wrong of the event that is named as a crime against humanity. To find a jurisdiction adequate to this task it has been necessary to expand what should count as our understanding of jurisdiction.

Hannah Arendt, for example, argued that international law and its tribunals build up our sense that crimes against humanity are an abuse against humanity and the very sense of an international legal order (Arendt 2006).[2] Paying attention to jurisdictional form might make us hesitate a little in formulating the wrong of crimes against humanity in terms of a wrong against legal order – at least in so far as it deflects from the reality of the wrong suffered. By locating a wrong in terms of an international order, as is done in international criminal law, we tend also to express the quality of the wrong as breaches of criminal and moral law. The institutions of law are rightly interested in many forms of ordering and orientation. However, they address the wrongdoer more than the wronged. As our brief analysis of the Eichmann trial showed, they engage with competing political, legal and moral interests, and so forth. Such competing interests can deflect from a just engagement with the wronged.

If we direct attention to the event or activity that called the jurisdiction into existence, the wrongs are not abstract, they are particular wrongs associated with the lives lived in relation with others. It is these wrongs that are the concern of the community which shares their lives through international criminal law. In this light an indictment should be understood as a calling to account – a calling for someone to answer for their actions (Duff 2010). It is a call authorised, if at all, by our sense of shared humanity. This is so despite all the difficulties of bringing an international community into forms of human relation. It is not only the wrongdoer who must answer for the wrong, so too must the community which shares their lives through a concern with the wrong (Gaita 1999).

Conclusion

In this chapter, we have discussed events as represented in two jurisdictional engagements, one emphasising the quality, plurality and rivalry of jurisdictions in the formation of the modern international, and the other addressing the ways in which new events might create or initiate new forms of jurisdiction. The first meeting was represented as political-legal and diplomatic. It stressed the ways in which the work of decolonisation has shaped forms of international engagement and civil forms of jurisdiction. The international community represented in this jurisdictional form was cast between two jurisdictional accounts of the international – one emphasised the free meeting of equal states in a new civil order, while the other imagined new states joining an already existing international order subject to forms of international law and government. The second jurisdictional engagement proceeded in response to the genocide of Jews by the Nazis. There we noted that the representation of genocide was divided between the territorial jurisdiction of the nation state and an international jurisdiction relating to war crimes. In this chapter we have investigated the ways in which the practices of jurisdiction have authorised and represented and given shape to the international domain as a series of institutions, events and activities. Part of the work of the jurist and critic is to find a jurisdictional idiom adequate to the task of representing events.

Notes

1   It is for these reasons that the basis of jurisdiction cannot be the passive personality principle.
2   The sense that a wrong or a crime is a crime against the authority of law is deeply embedded in criminal law. It reflects the sense that criminal law is an element of public law and concerns wrongs not only against individuals but against the state. International criminal law inherits this structure – hence the wrong against the international order.

References

Anghie, T. (2005) *Imperialism, Sovereignty and the Making of International Law*, Cambridge: Cambridge University Press.

Arendt, H. (2006) *Eichmann in Jerusalem: A Report on the Banality of Evil*, Harmondsworth: Penguin Books.

Black, C., McVeigh, S. and R. Johnstone (2007) 'Of the South', *Griffith Law Review* 16: 299–309.

Chatterjee, P. (1993) *Nationalist Thought and The Colonial World: A Derivative Discourse*, Tokyo: Zed Books.

Chimni, B. (2006) 'Third World Approaches to International Law: A Manifesto', *International Community Law Review* 8: 3–27.

Cowles, W. (1945) 'Universality of Jurisdiction over War Crimes', *California Law Review* 33: 181–194.

Cover, R. (1993) 'The Folktales of Justice: Tales of Jurisdiction', in Minow, M.,

Ryan, M. and Sarat, A. (eds), *Narrative, Violence and the Law: The Essays of Robert Cover*, Ann Arbor, MI: University of Michigan Press.

de Sousa Santos, B. and Rodriguez-Garavito, C. (eds) (2005) *Law and Globalisation from Below: Towards a Cosmopolitan Legality*, Cambridge: Cambridge University Press.

Duff, A. (2010) 'Authority and Responsibility in International Criminal Law', in Besson, S. and Tasioulas, J. (eds), *Philosophy of International Law*, Oxford: Oxford University Press.

Eslava, L. and Pahuja, S. (2011) 'Between Resistance and Reform: TWAIL and the Universality of International Law', *Trade, Law and Development* 3: 103–130.

Gaita, R. (1999) *A Common Humanity*, Melbourne: Text Publishing.

Glenn, P. (2010) *Legal Traditions of the World: Sustainable Diversity in Law*, 4th edn, New York, NY: Oxford University Press.

Grotius, H. (2005) *The Rights of War and Peace*, Book II, Indianapolis, IN: Liberty Fund.

Hobbes, R. (1968) *Leviathan*, Harmondsworth: Penguin.

Hossain, K. (1984) 'Introduction', in Hossain, K. and Chowdhury, S. (eds), *Permanent Sovereignty over Natural Resources in International Law: Principles and Practice*, London: Frances Pinter.

Hunter, I. (2001) *Rival Enlightenments: Civil and Metaphysical Philosophy in Early Modern Germany*, Cambridge: Cambridge University Press.

Hunter, I. (2010) 'Global Justice and Regional Metaphysics: On the Critical History of the Law of Nature and Nations', in Dorsett, S. and Hunter, I. (eds), *Law and Politics in British Colonial Thought: Transpositions of Empire*, New York, NY: Palgrave Macmillan.

Mann, I. (2010) 'The Dual Foundation of Universal Jurisdiction: Towards a Jurisprudence for the Court of Critique', *Transnational Legal Theory* 1: 485–521.

McVeigh, S. and Pahuja, S. (2009) 'Rival Jurisdictions: The Promise and Loss of Sovereignty', in Barbour, C. and Pavlich G. (eds), *After Sovereignty: On the Question of Political Beginnings*, London: Routledge.

Minson, J. (2009) 'In the Office of Humanity', *Cromohs* 14: 1–19.

Onuma, Y. (2000) 'When was the Law of International Society Born? – an Inquiry of the History of International Law from an Intercivilisational Perspective', *Journal of the History of International Law* 2: 1–66.

Orford, A. (2001) 'Globalisation and the Right to Development', in Alson, P. (ed), *People's Rights*, New York, NY: Oxford University Press.

Orford, A. (2011) *International Authority and the Responsibility to Protect*, Cambridge: Cambridge University Press.

Pagden, A. (1998) *Lords of All the World: Ideologies of Empire in Spain, Britain and France c. 1500 to c. 1800*, New Haven, CT: Yale University Press.

Pahuja, S. (2011a) 'Decolonisation and the Eventness of International Law', in Johns, F., Joyce, R. and Pahuja, S. (eds), *Events: The Force of International Law*, London: Routledge.

Pahuja, S. (2011b) *Decolonising International Law: Development, International Growth and the Politics of Universality*, Cambridge: Cambridge University Press.

Pogge, T. (2005) 'Recognized and Violated by International Law: The Human Rights of the Global Poor', *Leiden Journal of International Law* 18: 717–745.

Pufendorf, S., von (2009) *Two Books of the Elements of Universal Jurisprudence* (Oldfather, W. trans, 1931; Behme, T. ed), Indianapolis, IN: Liberty Fund.

Rajagopal, B. (2003) *International Law from Below: Development, Social Movements and Third World Resistance*, Cambridge: Cambridge University Press.

Shapcott, R. (2010) *International Ethics: A Critical Introduction*, Cambridge: Polity Press.

Chapter 8

Conclusions: responsibility and the forms of law

In an idiomatic sense, jurisdiction offers us the means and manner of articulating and expressing lawful relations. In this final chapter, we return to the offices of jurist, jurisprudent and critic in order to deepen the account of responsibility for the form of law. The critical approach to law presented here has been shaped around the ways in which it is possible to take responsibility for law by attending to the practices of jurisdiction. In particular we have paid attention to the ways in which thinking with jurisdiction through office shapes the forms of engagement of lawful relations. In doing so, we have not presented a general theory of law, or of jurisdiction, rather we have marshalled the repertoires of jurisdiction into a form of jurisprudence – a way of approaching law as a technology or as a material engagement of lawful relations.

The work of jurisdiction has been elaborated across three registers – the forms of jurisdictional authority, the technologies that create and maintain lawful relations, and the quality of lawful relationships. As with much else in this book, the question of authority has been expressed in terms of the ideas and the institutional repertoires of the common law tradition. As a matter of jurisprudence, we have sought to pluralise accounts of jurisdiction in order to open space for a consideration of forms of authority. The second register through which jurisdiction has been addressed was that of the technologies and repertoires of jurisdiction. Here, jurisdiction was presented in terms of the shaping of lawful relations through such material technologies as writing, mapping, precedent and categorisation. The third register in which we addressed jurisdiction was that of the quality of lawful relations. We suggested that questions of the practice of jurisdiction be considered in terms of a human measure – the quality of human relationship.

It is with the ethic of office and the responsibility of form that we close this book. Jurisdiction, as we have argued, creates forms of lawful relations and forms of responsibility for law. We have addressed this already in the context of the formation of the international community and in terms of the responsibility of the jurist and jurisprudent. We turn here to questions of responsibility for jurisdictional form. For some, this will be a step beyond law and jurisdiction. In a sense, this is right: responsibility is pre-eminently a matter of ethics and politics. However, if the argument we have presented carries weight, then jurisdictional practices also engage the political form of community and the acknowledgement of common humanity.

For the most part, questions of jurisdiction are addressed from the standpoint of the author or subject of law. We are used, within the university at least, to adopting the position of the sovereign, legislator or expert in legal order. However, the question of responsibility, it could be imagined, also belongs to the person who hears the law. Contemporary jurisprudence has obsessively linked judgment to the theory and practice of interpretation and to the justification of the legal order. Here, we treat the responsibility of law as part of the work of jurisdiction. Thus in this final chapter, we return to the major themes of this book: authority, technology and the forms of lawful relations. We do so in order to further or deepen an ethic of responsibility of jurisdictional idioms.

Authority

In this book, the question of authority has been addressed in terms of the inauguration and maintenance of lawful relations. We saw in earlier chapters some of the ways in which the political and legal exercise of authority has come to be shaped around the practice of sovereign/nation/ territory. Approaching authority through jurisdiction has allowed us to displace the centrality of accounts of sovereignty – and of accounts of responsibility shaped on territorial sovereignty. Jurisdiction, we have argued, offers one way of re-describing sovereign relations without leaving the domain of law and politics.

So how then should we characterise jurisdiction in terms of responsibility? In earlier chapters, we have offered an account of jurisdiction that stressed the way in which jurisdiction creates lawful relations. Rather than link jurisdiction to sovereign authority and the authority of power and command, we have emphasised an array of ways in which lawful relations have been engaged through jurisdictional practices. If we return for a moment to the 'diction' or speech of jurisdiction, jurisdiction gives us one way of addressing how authority emerges or coheres as law. A jurisdictional account of authority allows us to respond to such questions as: 'How does jurisdiction (and so law) take form?' and 'What utterance inaugurates a jurisdiction and establishes a power to legislate in its act of speech?'. For Costas Douzinas, for example, such questions of jurisdiction do not simply have answers in the history of law and practice, but rather form a part of the 'interior' sovereignty of law (Douzinas 2007: ch 11). Posing questions of jurisdiction in this manner might allow us to consider the ways in which it is possible to elaborate the repertoires of a response to law, of listening to law (Parker 2011). For Douzinas, what is important about jurisdiction is that through it we can track how the sovereign and the community expresses its law or authority. Jurisdiction here gives form to a new beginning (Arendt 1961). If this is so, then the question of jurisdiction also grants a privileged point of location for thinking about the site and point of determination of political and legal action.

We will briefly mention three further accounts of jurisdiction and authority that deepen the range of lawful relations addressed through idioms of jurisdiction. While somewhat different in idiom, the work of Robert Cover and Maria Drakopoulou draw out another theme of the inauguration or expression of jurisdiction: the way that jurisdiction is bound to violence and justice. For Cover (1993a), communities are created around *nomoi* (normative universes). He also notes, however, that the task of ordering law brings with it forms of (imperial) violence. For Maria Drakopoulou, the violence that engenders jurisdiction is shaped around sexual difference. The founding myths of jurisdiction involve the securing of (male) authority through the sacrifice of daughters (Drakopoulou 2007). This is the shape of the law that we inhabit.[1]

Douzinas, Cover and Drakopoulou all emphasise jurisdiction as the inauguration of law and the authority of law. Hannah Arendt, whose work we have discussed, reminds us that the relationship between the inaugural quality of jurisdiction, its newness, and the sense that a jurisdiction is authorised, or given, is not one that is settled or static (Arendt 1961). For Arendt, our understanding of authority and jurisdiction is always an understanding sought in the middle of events. As we note at the beginning of the book, for Arendt, authority is concerned with the creation of a space of political action and legal judgment that falls between, and joins, persuasion and force. We speak the law with authority, we are bound to law by obligation, we encounter other laws in response to our own. Treating the authority of law as a form of jurisdictional practice allows us to think of authority in terms of forms of conduct of community – of speakers and listeners – joined, however inadequately, through jurisdiction. For Arendt this is precisely the question of freedom that shapes the work of politics. A practice of responsibility requires, in some respect, a presence and response to others (Arendt 1961; Raz 2009).

Our second theme of authority can be stated more succinctly. The variety and plurality of legal forms alerts us to the many different forms of authority and modes of authorisation of lawful relations. Once authority and sovereign authority have been loosened from the inevitability of the jurisdictional alignment of state/territory/nation, it becomes possible to consider relations between jurisdictions, forms of law and lawfulness in different ways.

For Robert Cover (Cover 1993b), as for Douzinas, the point of engagement of law lies with the formation of normative universes (*nomoi*). State law is but one, imperial, form of law. The acknowledgement of the plurality of jurisdictional forms creates an ethic of responsibility that must attend to that plurality. In Chapter 2, we considered some older jurisdictional forms that were at the centre of both religious and political thinking about forms of civil society and the politics of state transformation (Hirst 1989).

In this book, our approach has not been to 'overcome' or 'transcend' the authority of law – or of the common law. Rather, we have tried to reinvest in – or inherit again – earlier forms of authority. Our critical approach to law, and to the form of law, has been directed towards finding technical forms through which it is possible to take responsibility for, and authorise, lawful relations. The wager of this book has been that there can be no talk of legal authority without jurisdiction, and no authorisation of law without an understanding of the technologies of jurisdiction. For some of the critics we have discussed, taking responsibility for office would involve the work of transcending or transforming law. Revolutionary, eschatological or indigenous jurisdictions may simply refuse the accounts of modes of authorisation of jurisdiction that have been considered in previous chapters.

Technology

In the body of this book, we have examined the technologies of jurisdiction and the way they create and arrange lawful relations. To do this, we considered how technologies of jurisdiction work to craft, and thus give form to, law. This approach emphasised jurisdiction as a practice of law. Here, as with the forms of authority, we reprise our investigation of technologies of jurisdiction by considering some of the forms of responsibility that arise with the crafting of lawful relations.

Our framing of the technologies of jurisdiction points to two distinct ways of thinking about institutions and the institutions of law. In one direction, we have investigated the technologies of jurisdiction as a means of assembling lawful relations. In another direction, we have investigated the ways in which technical means to attach or bind persons, places and events to the body of law. The rival traditions of jurisprudence and jurisdiction contest the significance, effect and affect of these procedures.

If jurisdictional practices create forms of lawful relation, a question arises as to how is it possible to take responsibility for these varied forms. Responding to this question would be one way of bringing the work of contemporary legal theory into relation with the work of jurisdiction. The work of Peter Goodrich has provided one way of sharpening accounts of the historical and ethical forms of responsibility associated with modern idioms of law. If, as we saw in Chapter 5, jurisdictional practices form or create subjects of law, then they also form or create patterns of responsibility available to those subjects. In his book, *Law in the Courts of Love*, Goodrich revives the 14th-century courts of love. Within literature, the courts of love adjudicated and disputed on matters of courtly love and on relations between men and women, spouses and lovers.[2] Goodrich addresses the literature on the courts of love as part of Renaissance *querelle des femmes*. However, this work is also an investigation into the variety of jurisdictional forms. Importantly, the courts provide a place for considering jurisdictional forms that would be adequate to the task of adjudicating between genders on matters of love. By concentrating on the plurality of forms of personal jurisdictions, then, it is possible to offer a critical account of the repertoires of lawful actions of persons. An account of jurisdiction must also offer an account of relations between persons of law (Parsley 2010).[3]

The formulation of jurisdiction in terms of territory represents the form of law in a particular way. As with a technology of persons, we return to the technologies of territorial jurisdiction in order to reconsider their form. As a way of engaging with the responsibility for a jurisdictional form, we addressed territory in terms of a jurisdiction of place and a meeting of laws. Aside from the political question of the formation of meeting places of law, this gave us both an account of the meeting of jurisdictions and a way of considering the repertoire of lawful relations. The question of the relation of law and place is the subject matter of several disciplines within the humanities. Geographers, historians and cultural theorists have all, in different ways, pointed to the particular relations of space and place created through legal relations. More often than not what is highlighted is the way in which forms of law de-materialise local relations in the name of the state, and the way in which the legal understanding of space differs from the lived experience of space and place (Lefebvre 1991; Butler 2012). For us, it is not just the meeting of laws which is important, but the ways in which those laws move in, and create, lawful place. The imperial movement of the common law around the world was the most important transmission of law in the 19th century. In the 20th century, it might be said to be the movement of international bureaux and armies that transmits law across the globe.

A jurisdiction gives place – a site from which to speak or proclaim the law and from which to form relations with the world. The work of Hannah Arendt, and of public artists like Paul Carter, reminds us that the meeting places of law are the work and responsibility of creation. Creation, however, is not simply abstract. Paul Carter, for example, looks to the ceremonial creation of the public sphere. The deliberative, adjudicatory, and commemorative aspects of jurisdiction are part of the creation of a public space (Carter 2008). Neglect these aspects of jurisdiction and it becomes difficult to engage and move with a community of law. To hold on to the critical responsibility of law, we could re-describe the concern with the loss of material form of law as one of the loss of the ceremonial performance of law. The ceremonial forms of the state ordering of common law are well known. The ceremonies of investiture and adjudication, and the symbolic representation of justice, all create relations of place and a community of laws. Just as sovereign territorial jurisdictions are not the only jurisdictional forms, so other jurisdictional forms also have their ceremonial arrangements. Here, ceremonial might include the continuing work of the repatriation of the indigenous dead to their law and land, or the ceremonial creation and engagement of new forms of civil relation, such as civil union or gay marriage. Another example might be the Universal Declaration of the Rights of Mother Earth (2010) which formulates a jurisdiction of the earth (Universal Declaration 2010).

Something of the difficulty of holding onto a jurisdiction of place capable of sustaining lawful relations is also to be found in thinking about the jurisdictional arrangement of events or activities. In earlier parts of the book, we considered some of the older forms of jurisdictional engagements structured around events. We found this useful in order to address different forms of authority, ordering and lawful relations. Our final engagement with technologies lies with the jurisdiction of events and activities. This we will discuss under the heading of freedom. A jurisdiction of events shapes forms of responsibility for freedom. As was seen in Chapter 7, the engagement of responsibility for events in the international domain has taken place through many different jurisdictions. We close our discussion of technology not with a reconsideration of forms of accountability for events, but with a brief consideration of the engagement of technology.

Anxiety or concern with forms of technology has formed a large part of the engagement of 19th- and 20th-century critical thinking. For critics writing in marxist traditions of critical thought, such as Herbert Marcuse, technical relations and legal ordering have alienated the social relations of people from their human nature, the worker from their work. Modern law, argues Evgeny Pashukanis, gives the world and life its form as commodity. Critics have worried too about how the formalities of law estrange or alienate us both from questions of domination, exploitation and suffering and the forms justice that might be capable of redressing such wrongs (Marcuse 1941; Pashukanis 1978; Williams 1991). Technical thinking, in short, is only about means and not about ultimate ends, and the forms of responsibility that engage such limited means are also limited. It might be thought then that the work of jurisdiction – even a universal jurisdiction – is precisely to turn attention away from ultimate ends in favour of finding determinate, or limited, forms of responsibility. Indeed many critics argue that technology and the technologies of law do turn us over to endless calculation and production. Law is an instrument of dispute and order. It forms part of the endless desire to master the globe (Douzinas and Geary 2005).

As we have concentrated on the way in which lawful relations are created through jurisdictional practices, we have accepted forms of limited ends. The technologies of the civil jurisdiction of the common law that we have discussed do not draw its subjects towards religious truth, but towards peace and civility. Those of the jurisdiction of conscience hold us to the subject of human rights and not radical forms of freedom. Events are taken into law or joined for a reason. In part, our reason for holding this formulation of jurisdiction has been quite pragmatic. We have not developed styles of jurisdictional engagement that address or criticise the form of law in its totality. Rather, we have worked with accounts of law that argue that legal relations are embedded in social and natural life. Law is a human artefact, its instruments and tools create forms of human relations.

Office and responsibility: lawful relations and freedom

Returning to the office of jurist and jurisprudent, we make our last formulations of responsibility for the form of law. While care for the practices of jurisdiction is not the only obligation of office, it is one of the more important responsibilities of the jurist, jurisprudent and critic. In developing our account of jurisdiction, or at least of a jurisdiction of the common law, we have offered six pointers to a critical approach to law through jurisdiction. Perhaps as befits an approach to the jurisdictional forms of the common law tradition, they are hybrid:

1. *Form/activity*. To approach law through jurisdiction is to approach law as an activity and a conduct of life. A form of law is a practice that has taken on shape and meaning in various ways. This can best be understood through the history and genealogy of jurisdictional forms.

2. *Authority*. An exercise of jurisdiction involves the creation and exercise of forms of lawful relation. We understand forms of legal authority through the mode and manner of their authorisation. Within common law idioms, authority falls somewhere between force and reason. The exercise or authorisation of authority gives us the form of jurisdiction and the patterns and relations of law. In so far as authority is not mired in tradition, it can be understood as the engagement with others (in amity or emnity) through action and opinion.

3. *Technology*. The technologies of jurisdiction craft or shape lawful relations. They both bind us to the institutions of law and establish the repertoires of lawful relations. They pattern our existence around relations of persons, places and events, and bind our engagement in the world to relations of conscience and civility.

4. *Conduct of lawful relations*. A jurisdiction creates the repertoires of lawful relations. A critical approach to law through jurisdiction follows the conduct of lawful relations. Within the common law tradition a jurisdiction or authority to act or create relations has been aligned with forms of dignity, status and office and modes of civility and conscience. This language also sustains much of the critical understanding of lawful relations. If a jurisdiction crafts lawful relations, then one part of a critical approach to law is to humanise lawful relations.

5. *Ethic of office*. The understanding of responsibility that most readily holds to forms of jurisdiction is shaped around an ethic of office. In

this book, the ethic of office has been ordered around the practice of humanising law and acknowledging forms of human measure and of common humanity. How this is done is as much a matter of acknowledging the limits of office as of the acknowledgement of human relations.

6.   *The critic*. For the critic, approaching law through jurisdiction is both a practical concern and a way of revealing what is most important to those who engage with lawful relations. Jurisdictional thinking addresses the ways in which we practise responsibility through lawful relations. This means addressing something like ultimate ends. Such ends, in so far as the common law traditions have the courage to address them, are framed in a language of authority and belong to the inheritance of a tradition. They circulate around the practice and understanding of freedom – here, freedom for responsibility (Wolcher 2004; Black 2011).

Redress

We return to one of the places from where we started in Chapter 1 – the work of the poet Seamus Heaney. There we addressed Seamus Heaney's phrase 'jurisdiction of form' from his essay 'Feeling into Words' (Heaney 2002). What we found important in that essay was how Heaney linked the crafting and technique of feeling directly to the achievement of a proper form. Following Heaney, a jurisprudence of jurisdiction becomes a preoccupation with the creation of the forms of law. We close this book with another phrase borrowed from Heaney, this time one relating to justice: redress (Heaney 1995).

Heaney characterises the redress of poetry in terms of a counterweight – a balancing out of forces (Heaney 1995). For Heaney, poetry offers to place 'a counter-reality in the scales', that is an imagined reality that can 'balance out against the historical situation' (Heaney 1995). Heaney's poetry has the task of bearing witness to what has been revealed. A critical jurisprudence, it might be imagined – whether it is directed towards redressing law or whether it is prospective and concerned with expressing a justice yet to come – is an attempt to 'balance out against the historical situation' or to redress the realities with which it is faced and surrounded. A jurisprudence of jurisdiction is an imagined engagement of law, and is one that should act as a kind of legal truth. Seamus Heaney describes the truths of poetry that are adequate to their task as 'bracing and memorable'. So too should a jurisprudence be if it brings law to life – however unlikely that may seem.

It must be said that the common law and its jurisprudence is an unlikely candidate to fulfil this task. Its civilities and beliefs have been as equally at home in colonial and post-colonial missions of order and civilisation as they were in the royal courts in England in the 17th century. However, in so far as we inherit, or continue to benefit from the jurisdictions of the common law, we still need to account for the forms of law. It continues to be necessary to ask 'Whose jurisdiction?' and 'Why this jurisdiction? – and it is still possible to address these questions through the call and redress of justice.

Notes

1   This theme is also explored in different ways in the work of Carole Pateman and Luce Irigaray. Carole Patemen points to the ways in which enlightenment political philosophy repeats this gesture in the transition from paternal authority of kingship to the fraternal authority of republics (Pateman 1988). Luce Irigaray points to the way in which modern Western law pronounces law from the standpoint and concerns of a male jurisdiction and not two jurisdictions, masculine and feminine (Irigaray 2007).
2   *Querelle des femmes* refers to the 'formulaic debate as to the place, social and natural status, education and deportment of women', one element of which traditionally was the idea that women were not wholly human. See Goodrich 1996: 117. For further on this, see Kelly 1984.
3   Although developed in a rather different idiom, the consequences of these formulations of jurisdiction are developed by Margaret Davies in terms of an .'intersectional feminism' (Davies 2008).

References

Arendt, H. (1961) *Between Past and Future: Six Exercises in Political Thought*, London: Faber.

Black, C.F. (2011) *The Land is the Source of the Law*, London: Routledge.

Butler, C. (2012) *Henri Lefebvre: Spatial Politics, Everyday Life and the Right to the City*, London: Routledge-Cavendish.

Carter, P. (2008) *Dark Writing: Geography, Performance, Design*, Honolulu: University of Hawai'i Press.

Cover, R. (1993a) 'The Folktales of Justice: Tales of Jurisdiction', in Minow, M., Ryan, M. and Sarat, A. (eds) *Narrative, Violence, and the Law: The Essays of Robert Cover*, Ann Arbor, MI: University of Michigan Press.

Cover, R. (1993b) 'Nomos and Narrative', in Minow, M., Ryan, M. and Sarat, A. (eds), *Narrative, Violence, and the Law: The Essays of Robert Cover*, Ann Arbor, MI: University of Michigan Press.

Davies, M. (2008) *Asking the Law Question*, 3rd edn, Sydney: Law Book Company.

Douzinas, C. (2007) *Human Rights and Empire: The Political Philosophy of Cosmopolitanism*, London: Taylor & Francis.

Douzinas, C. and Geary, A. (2005) *Critical Jurisprudence*, Oxford: Hart Publishing.

Drakopoulou, M. (2007) 'Of the Founding of Law's Jurisdiction and the Politics of Sexual Difference: the Case of Roman Law', in McVeigh, S. (ed), *Jurisprudence of Jurisdiction*, London: Routledge.

Goodrich, P. (1996) *Law in the Courts of Love: Literature and Other Minor Jurisprudences*, New York, NY: Routledge.

Heaney, S. (1995) *The Redress of Poetry: Oxford Lectures*, London: Faber & Faber.

Heaney, S. (2002) *Finders Keepers: Selected Prose 1971–2001*, London: Faber & Faber.

Hirst, P. (ed) (1989) *The Pluralist Theory of the State: Selected Writings of G. D. H. Cole, J. N. Figgis, and H. J. Laski*, London: Routledge.

Irigaray, L. (2007) *Je, Tu, Nous: Toward a Culture of Difference*, London: Routledge.

Kelly, J. (1984) 'Early Feminist Theory and the *Querelle des Femmes*', in Kelly, J. (ed) *Women, History and Theory: The Essays of Joan Kelly*, Chicago, IL: University of Chicago Press.

Lefebvre, H. (1991) *The Production of Space* (Nicholson-Smith, D. trans), Oxford: Basil Blackwell.

Marcuse, H. (1941) *Reason and Revolution*, New York, NY: Oxford University Press.

Parker, J. (2011) 'The Soundscape of Justice', *Griffith Law Review*, 20: 962–993.

Parsley, C. (2010) 'The Mask and Agamben: the Transitional Juridical Technics of Legal Relation', *Law Text Culture* 14(1): 12–39.

Pashukanis, E. (1978) *The General Theory of Law and Marxism* (Einhorn, B. trans), London: Ink Links.

Pateman, C. (1988) *The Sexual Contract*, Cambridge: Polity Press.

Raz, J. (2009) *The Authority of Law: Essays on Law and Morality*, 2nd edn, Oxford: Oxford University Press.

Universal Declaration (2010) Universal Declaration of the Rights of Mother Earth, Bolivia, Draft 2010, <http://motherearthrights.org/> (accessed 4 December 2011).

Williams, P. (1991) *The Alchemy of Race and Rights*, Cambridge, MA: Harvard University Press.

Wolcher, L. (2004) *The End of Technology: A Polemic, Washington Law Review* 79: 331–388.

Index